To Debra,
You're a great gal.
the faith.
Sencerely,
Shirley
July 18, 2004

WHERE IS MY SON JEFFREY?

THE TRUE STORY OF A MOTHER-IN-COMBAT

SHIRLEY MAYS

WHERE IS MY SON JEFFREY?

An Inside Story of Power, Greed, Drugs and Money Laundering

First published by AuthorHouse 06/16/04

ISBN: 1-4184-1573-1 (e-book)
ISBN: 1-4184-1574-X (Paperback)

This book is printed on acid free paper.

TABLE OF CONTENTS

DEDICATED TO PEOPLE

EVERYWHERE

WHO LIVE WITH THE UNKNOWN

INTRODUCTION

The purpose of this book is not to vent my anger, frustrations or resentments and not to personally hurt anyone, but to warn you, the public, that this same situation could happen to you. If I can be one of the messengers to sound the alarm, then my efforts have been worth it. After reading and rereading the depositions and trial transcripts of this Neimay lawsuit for the first time since 1991, I truly believe it is my responsibility to tell you this story which is based on facts.

Corporate corruption is rampant in our country. We have a few very strong leaders trying to do something about it. I believe that each and every one of us has a responsibility to *STAND UP AND BE COUNTED*. We are either part of the problem or part of the solution. That choice is ours. Or we can sit on the fence. That is also our choice.

My fight is against white-collar crime. Specifically real estate white-collar crime. Specifically on the Outer Banks of North Carolina. It takes real estate brokers, lawyers, bankers and accountants working together to accomplish this. You can't blame one without the other.

All of the characters in this book have a fiduciary responsibility to the public. Many of them are failing miserably. Many of them are still going full speed. They are reflecting badly on their professions.

My facts are based on the depositions taken from the executor, the CPA, the banker, the partnership attorney and a three-day transcript of the Neimay trial.

It is my deep belief that one must clean up his or her backyard before they have a right to complain about others.

I am a North Carolina real estate broker. The OUTER BANKS OF NORTH CAROLINA happens to be my backyard. My goal is to help clean it up. I challenge the honest lawyers, bankers, accountants and realtors of the Outer Banks to do the same.

Set an example. Maybe it will be contagious.

CAST OF CHARACTERS

FISHERMEN
>EDGAR STYRON, JR.
>JOCK MCKENZIE

FEDERAL GOVERNMENT

UNITED STATES DEPARTMENT OF JUSTICE
>Supervisory Special Agent, FBI

DEPARTMENT OF THE TREASURY
>Suzanne Battles, Informant Claims, IRS

STATE OF NORTH CAROLINA

NORTH CAROLINA DEPARTMENT OF JUSTICE
>Lacy H. Thornburg, Attorney General
>Rodney Maddox, Special Assistant to the Attorney General

STATE BUREAU OF INVESTIGATIONS
>Charles Dunn, Director
>Melinda C. Coffin, Special Agent, Financial Crime
Investigations

NORTH CAROLINA STATE BOARD OF CPA EXAMINERS
>Executive Director
>Coordinator of Professional Standards

NORTH CAROLINA BANKING COMMISSION
>Special Assistant to the Commissioner of Banks

NORTH CAROLINA STATE AUDITOR'S OFFICE
>Fraud and Abuse Supervisor

NORTH CAROLINA REAL ESTATE COMMISSION
Deputy Legal Counsel

NORTHEASTERN NORTH CAROLINA

SUPERIOR COURT JUDGES
George M. Fountain, Trial Judge, Superior Court Judge
Herbert Small, Senior Superior Court Judge
Thomas Watts, Superior Court Judge
Charles B. Winberry, Superior Court Judge
Russell Duke, Superior Court Judge

DISTRICT ATTORNEY
H. P. Williams, Jr, District Attorney, First Prosecutorial District

CLERK OF COURT
Betty S. Mann, Clerk of Superior Court, Dare County, NC

PLANTERS NATIONAL BANK
President, Rocky Mount, NC
Asst. Legal Counsel, Rocky Mount, NC
W. Ray White, President, Manteo, NC
S. Chris Payne, Vice President, Manteo, NC
Wilson Shearin, Asst. Vice President, Manteo, NC

PEOPLES BANK
Trust Officer, Rocky Mount, NC

ATTORNEYS
Norman W. Shearin, Jr., Kitty Hawk, NC
Thomas L White, Jr.
> Kellogg, White, Evans, Sharp and Michael, Manteo, NC

Benita A. Lloyd
> Kellogg, White, Evans, and Gray, Manteo, NC

NEIMAY LIMITED PARTNERSHIP

GENERAL PARTNER
George W. Neighbors, Kitty Dunes Realty, Kitty Hawk, NC

LIMITED PARTNER
Harold B. Mays, Ligonier, Pennsylvania

PARTNERSHIP ATTORNEYS
Norman W. Shearin, Jr., Original Neimay Attorney, Kitty Hawk, NC
> Trustee for Pauline Woodard, Peoples Bank, Rocky Mount, NC

Thomas L. White, Jr.,
> Kellogg, White, Evans, Sharp and Michael, Manteo, NC

PARTNERSHIP ACCOUNTANTS
Jasper L. Adams, Original Neimay Accountant, Southern Shores, NC

Debbie J. Burgess, Johnson, Burgess and Adams Firm
> Southern Shores, NC

PLAINTIFF ATTORNEY
John S. Morrison, Elizabeth City, NC

DEFENSE ATTORNEY
O. C. Abbott, Elizabeth City, NC

EXECUTOR of The Estate of George W. Neighbors
John B. Neighbors, son and real estate broker, Kitty Hawk, NC

PLAINTIFF'S AGENT
Shirley L. Mays, agent of plaintiff and author

The true story you are about to read involves a woman who has taken on white-collar crime with the vengeance of a mother-in-combat. It involves prominent lawyers, bankers, accountants, real estate brokers and of course, sea captains. The names are real and the facts are well documented.

CHAPTER 1

A SHORT FAMILY HISTORY

Let me introduce myself.

I am a mother of three – one son and two daughters. My oldest child and only son Jeffrey has been missing for 23 years. He was barely 21 years old. I live with the hope that he is alive somewhere in the world. He and another young man of the same age disappeared on November 13, 1980 at 1:30 p.m. 16 miles off the Coast of Cape Hatteras. They simply went fishing and never came home.

We were a happy, all American family. My husband, Harold B. (Bud) Mays was a very successful young entrepreneur. He and a partner started a business in the early 70's in Latrobe, Pennsylvania. It was one of those garage stories where you make it by night and sell it by day. It became a very successful national business. It was a xerographic business, now owned by Pelican, a German company.

In 1974, my husband sold out to his partner. We received a down payment on the sale of the Latrobe business and we needed to reinvest the money. We had, in the past, invested mostly in real estate. We had done quite well with our investments, so it was natural for us to head to the Kitty Hawk area and see what was up in that real estate world.

We were one of a few privileged people on the East Coast who owned a Coast Guard Station – *The Kitty Hawk Coast Guard Station in Kitty Hawk, North Carolina*. It was our summer home and we loved it! It was our favorite place in the entire world. We had bought it in 1970 from a dear friend of my family.

SHIRLEY MAYS

It was the winter of 1974. In those years, not many folks ventured to the Outer Banks in the cold months. I have always loved the beach and enjoyed being there when it was not overrun with tourists.

It was quite natural that I would spot a real estate sign, being pushed into the sand, just a short distance from our Station. The sign read – "Tract of Land (45 acres), Ocean to Sound, Estate Property, Contact Peoples Bank." I knew the area quite well. I had grown up at the Outer Banks since I was seven. My family had one of the first motels in Nags Head. They built it in the early 40's. I had watched the area grow and I thought I had a good feel for the development of it. This was to me, an exceptional tract of land.

Before we called the bank, we stopped to see a Kitty Hawk realtor. His company was KITTY DUNES and his name was George Neighbors. We had been living in Pennsylvania for about 12 years. I wasn't familiar with all of the new names in Kitty Hawk. We thought we would mention the property and see what his opinion was on that particular tract of land. He appeared very shocked and said that the bank was suppose to let him know first because he had developed the piece right next to that tract. It was called Kitty Dunes South. He asked us if we were interested in developing that particular tract with him.

We checked him out and everyone we talked to seemed to like him. He was a "foreigner" from Maryland. He seemed nice enough. He appeared to be a laid back person.

ANYWAY, as we say in the South, we put up the money and became the ***limited partner*** and he put up the "goodwill" and became the ***general partner*** in a partnership called NEIMAY – a combination of Neighbors and Mays. The development became Kitty Dunes West (Oceanside), Kitty Dunes Commercial (Bypass), Kitty Dunes Annex and Kitty Dunes Village (Soundside).

This is a classic example of how smart, hard working people can walk into a flimflam real estate deal. This is somewhat parallel to a real estate deal in Arkansas called WHITEWATER Our **general partner** died – instead of going to prison – and we had a fighting chance of pulling out of the mess.

I have to be very careful that I don't get ahead of myself with this story. *Of course,* I am telling it in retrospect. If I bounced back and forth the way it really happened, you would not be able to follow me. I am going to try to stay focused on my son Jeffrey and the Neimay Partnership. I have had enough happen to me in the last 23 years for my mind to explode. I am going to try real hard not to get into the many, many other things that were happening to me at the same time.

We became partners with this Eastern Shore gentleman from Maryland and my husband trusted him. I immediately began to doubt him. I'm sure it was my God given instinct kicking in. I could tell he didn't really like me around. There was just something that was too comfortable about him. I made my feelings known to my husband but he thought I just didn't *trust* people enough.

We were smart enough to keep our lawyer and our accountant of many years from Pittsburgh, Pennsylvania. We knew we were getting the best professional opinions from them. With that comfort level in mind, I thought to myself "how much trouble can we get into?"

We lived in Ligonier, Pennsylvania at the time – a beautiful little town where our children grew up. In retrospect, I now know that George Neighbors liked to deal with partners who lived "out of the area" – which we did – at *that* time.

In 1977 our only son, Jeffrey, graduated from Ligonier High School and decided he wanted to move to the South and go to school at East Carolina College in Greenville, North Carolina. Of course, one of his main reasons was to be near the Coast Guard Station – the summer home that he loved so much. The other reason and not a small one was to be near his devoted maternal grandparents and relatives who lived in Camden, North Carolina – a hop skip from both Greenville and Kitty Hawk. Jeffrey *loves* family and the area very much and simply wanted to be a part of it.

4

At the same time, we decided to move back to my hometown of Elizabeth City, North Carolina – a short distance from Camden, Kitty Hawk and *Greenville*. The winters were harsh in Pennsylvania and since my husband had sold his business, we really could live anywhere we wanted. To tell the honest truth, I didn't mind being a little closer to East Carolina College. We packed up and moved to my hometown of Elizabeth City, North Carolina in the summer of 1977. Elizabeth City is about 45 minutes from our Station. *Life appeared to be great*.

When my husband sold his Latrobe business, he retained his spin-off business in Los Angeles. He had been bored since selling his main manufacturing plant so he spent a lot of time in L. A. with that partner. The West Coast business involved the selling of toner, paper and other office products. I thought we would just retire from the business world but lo and behold, my husband decided to move the West Coast business to Elizabeth City. In a phone call from California, he suggested that I buy a building, buy a house in Elizabeth City and sell the Pennsylvania house because he was bringing the business to the East Coast – lock, stock and barrel – in November.

This was the summer of 1977. The children and I were living and playing at the beach in our summer home. All of a sudden, we had a new direction. I went to work – buying a building – buying a house - and selling a house! With all of that accomplished, he moved the business across the country in November 1977 and we were in a new time of life.

GEORGE NEIGHBORS NEVER THOUGHT WE WOULD BE MOVING TO THE AREA. I FIRMLY BELIEVE NOW IF HE HAD, HE WOULD NOT HAVE GONE INTO BUSINESS WITH US. I WAS LATER TOLD THAT HIS STYLE WAS TO GO INTO BUSINESS WITH LITTLE OLD LADIES IN OTHER STATES WHO DON'T ASK QUESTIONS.

After moving to the area, my husband would go to Kitty Hawk a lot and just chew the fat with George. They got to be good buddies – he thought. My husband didn't ask a lot of business questions or look at the books because he trusted George. George always told him how great everything was going and how much money both of them would make on this real estate venture.

We needed an accountant for our new Elizabeth City business so George suggested Jack Adams, the CPA who followed him to the Outer Banks. Adams was the Neimay Partnership's personal and only accountant so I felt sure he must be qualified. Adams came to Elizabeth City. After a few days, I realized *he didn't* know what he was doing. We flew in our CPA from Pittsburgh. Our CPA from Pittsburgh was surprised because the books were simple. Adams willingly left town charging us nothing. I had my doubts about him from that day forward. I am now aware that Jack Adams is mostly a "creative" accountant. As a matter of fact, I was told he later lost his license because of his creativity.

After about three years into our new business venture in Elizabeth City, my husband came home one day and said he had been to Kitty Hawk and George, ***the general partner*** and real estate broker, told him he had a business for sale that was "one of a kind." It was an old established fish market and grocery store called NUNEMAKERS. I knew Charles Nunemaker from my younger years at the beach with my family. My family had owned businesses for years at the Outer Banks. I immediately cautioned my husband of the aches and pains of owning a seasonal business at the beach and the reasons my family sold out and came back to the Elizabeth City area. After owning and running his Pennsylvania business, which was a national one, he needed more of a challenge than running a business in a small town. He definitely got that challenge.

George Neighbors made a big sale and Nunemakers became another business of ours. Charles Nunemaker sold his retail store to us, and kept his wholesale fish business - both named Nunemaker after him. At the time my husband went to the beach to run his new business, I "inherited" the management of the Elizabeth City businesses. That was in June 1980.

Our son Jeffrey loved the beach and dearly loved fishing and hunting. It was quite natural for him to be excited about us buying this established fish business. We made him a partner in Nunemakers Retail. He left Greenville and moved to the beach and went to work at the fish company. He was truly a happy camper.

On November 13, 1980 – a few short months after joining the business, Jeffrey and another young man, who was working for us, went fishing off the Coast of Cape Hatteras in the Gulf Stream. We bought him a Sea Ox because we believed it to be a very seaworthy boat. The fish business was hurting and it appeared the only way you could survive was to catch your own fish. The boys went out early that morning and never returned.

It was "reported" that day by one Edgar Styron, Jr. and his buddy Jock McKenzie that the boys had developed a freeze plug problem. It was "reported" by Edgar Styron that he whittled them a plug. These two gentlemen were the last to see Jeffrey and his friend. It was "reported" by Edgar Styron, Jr. to the Coast Guard rescue that they then were seen speeding away. It was "reported" by Edgar Styron, Jr. to Coast Guard rescue that he tried to catch them because they were heading in the wrong direction. So much for Edgar Styron, Jr.'s "reporting" anything to anybody. I would venture to say that nobody – and I mean nobody - will ever really know what happened that fateful day 16 miles offshore except Edgar Styron, Jr., his buddy Jock McKenzie – and of course, Jeffrey and his friend.

There was a long, long, sad, sad, sea hunt. I'm told it was one of the biggest ever on the East Coast. *I don't believe the boys perished at sea.*

I have reason to believe my son is alive somewhere in the world. I have spent the last 23 years of my life looking for him. He is in my prayers day and night.

At that time in 1980, there was a lot of international drug dealing off the Coast of Cape Hatteras. It was fueled by the tremendous corruption going on within our country and specifically within my home state of North Carolina and even more specific, within the area of the Outer Banks of Dare County, North Carolina.

A lot of that drug money went into Outer Banks businesses and real estate.

I have reason to believe that November 13, 1980 might have been one of those drug days. I believe the boys were in the wrong place at the wrong time.

For the last 23 years, I have had an abnormal drive in my personal fight against any corruption that remotely surrounded my son Jeffrey that fateful day.

It takes a lot to keep me busy. I despise drugs. I despise corruption. I despise what it might do to my daughters and grandchildren. I despise what it is doing to many families like us. I despise the fact that our family has had to live with the unknown for over 23 years. I really despise what all of this is doing to our country.

From 1983 to 1991, I pursued a real estate white-collar crime. I was told that it was one of the longest and biggest paper cases ever in Dare County. I feel that we were royally sandbagged by the absolute disregard for justice in the judicial system of District 1 of Northeastern North Carolina. If justice delayed is justice denied, then we were truly denied justice.

George Neighbors, our **general partner** in Neimay, passed away on July 25, 1983 from cancer. Immediately after George's death, we became concerned about our future position and possible liability in the Neimay partnership. My husband and I went to Manteo, North Carolina to meet with our partnership attorney, Thomas W. White, Jr. of the Kellogg, White, Evans, Sharp and Michael firm. This was a very prominent firm not only in Manteo but also in the State of North Carolina. We expected nothing but the best legal advice from him.

During that meeting, Tom White started talking in legal circles as to why we *couldn't* take over control of the partnership. This was contrary to what it said in our partnership papers, which had been given the seal of approval by our own Pennsylvania lawyer. Besides, in North Carolina a partnership automatically dissolves at the death of either partner. We couldn't understand his strange actions. He appeared nervous. We even called our personal attorney, John Morrison in Elizabeth City, and put Tom White on the phone. John didn't understand Tom's concerns either but nobody seemed to be able to change his mind.

In March of 1985, after diligently trying for two years to get the records that were legally ours – and after every effort was made to work with the lawyers, bankers, accountants and the son and executor of George Neighbors – a lawsuit was filed. At that time Bud Mays was still legally the *limited partner*, so the lawsuit was filed in his name and I became the *PLAINTIFF'S AGENT.*

We were a family trying to survive the loss of our son. My husband lost interest in everything. He decided he wanted to sell Nunemakers and move back to Ligonier, Pennsylvania. I was still running the businesses in Elizabeth City and trying every day just to keep my sanity. I asked him to please let us split some properties so I might have a chance to survive financially. At that time, he wasn't even trying to tread water. My son was missing too. I had a hard time feeling sorry for anyone else at that moment in my life. We split properties and my husband left for Ligonier on the afternoon of my father's funeral in July of 1985.

When Bud and I split properties in June of 1985, he signed over the Neimay partnership to me. *I inherited "the Neimay boys" at that time.*

My story is about a real estate scam by a developer who, to my knowledge, was one of the first flimflammers on the Outer Banks of North Carolina. It involves a cover-up by lawyers, bankers, accountants and the executor after his death. It's very, very difficult to prove fraud against prominent people like lawyers, bankers and accountants because they work together so well. You can prove deception – unethical behavior – and definitely sloppy bookkeeping but they usually cover themselves just short of fraud.

If it were not for the O.J. Simpson trial, I am not sure I would have tackled this book. The average citizen did not understand the judicial system of this country at that time.

9

I now believe the American public, if not the world, has become more educated as to the workings of our judicial system. We, the public, are more knowledgeable about motions and orders; the sustaining and overruling of the presentation of evidence; the importance of documented evidence; the constitutional right of a fair and speedy trial and what I believe is the most important benefit of all – THE RIGHT TO A JURY. Even though the judicial system is in shambles, at least we still have the right to a jury. I believe in the American people even though I've temporarily lost hope in the American Judicial System.

Unfortunately I didn't have the legal understanding of matters back in 1985 that I have now about the right to a jury. The legal advice I was given then by John Morrison, our attorney for the Neimay lawsuit, was that it would be better for a judge to hear our case because a jury wouldn't understand the accounting of it.

That was probably decent advice - if you're lucky enough to get a judge who understands accounting.

When the case began to get delayed, delayed, and delayed by the lawyers and accountants who were not producing the discovery, I then insisted on a jury because the fair and speedy opportunity was gone. We were then DENIED a jury by the judge. *Why would he do that*? I learned, at that time, if you don't ask for one in the beginning, it is at the discretion of the judge who happens to be "riding the circuit" at the time. That's the way it is – in North Carolina – at least in Northeastern North Carolina. I certainly had to learn the hard way that you are not *always* allowed a jury.

We had been begging for discovery since 1983. I was amazed when we finally got to court in 1991.

Two judges refused to hear the case. *Just didn't want to hear it.* A very good Republican judge was finally assigned. John did a lot of research on him and we were very pleased that we might have a chance of a fair trial.

WRONG!

The morning of the first day of the trial, a different judge showed up! My attorney went into shock when he saw him. He said, "Oh my God, it's Shoot From the Hip George Fountain." We had no advance notice at all. We had an "outside" judge who had been sent to Manteo, North Carolina to hear this case.

RIGHT THEN, I KNEW WE WERE IN TROUBLE. I JUST DIDN'T KNOW HOW MUCH!

I am writing this book specifically because *I don't think we got a fair trial.*

Our attorney, John Morrison, ran scared – real scared. He should have been more concerned about the involvement of the two main banks that Neimay dealt with - Planters National Bank in Manteo, NC and Peoples Bank and Trust Company in Rocky Mount, NC. John was on a small retainer with Peoples and had his office in their Elizabeth City branch. We started this lawsuit in March of 1985. Six years later, at the time of trial, the two banks had merged. I kept asking John if he had a conflict of interest because of his retainer with Peoples. I have, in writing, he consistently said no. By the time of trial, the merger had become Centura Bank. It is now RBC Centura Bank (Royal Bank of Canada).

I asked for an appeal immediately after the trial was over. John was hard to find and hard to push at that point. Some new legislation had been enacted and the loophole used to get him away from me was that he was three days late in filing the appeal. He filed and then notified me that he was withdrawing from the appeal.

We couldn't find justice in THAT judicial system so I am going to do what I should have done for the last 12 or 13 years. I am going to bring the facts to you, the real jury, the COURT OF PUBLIC OPINION.

The story I am about to tell is solidly documented and I will tell it as plainly as I can and to the best of my knowledge. Our judicial rights were shattered but thank God, I still retain my constitutional rights of Freedom of Speech and Freedom of the Press.

Because of these rights, it is my honor and privilege to *once again* present this case –and this time to you, the public.

YOU ARE MY JURY

CHAPTER 2

NEIMAY LIMITED PARTNERSHIP HISTORY

Neimay Limited Partnership was formed May 24th, 1975 in an agreement drawn up by Norman W. Shearin, Jr. an attorney-at-law whose office was in Kitty Hawk, North Carolina He was replaced in 1977 by Thomas L. White, Jr. of Kellogg, White, Evans, Sharp and Michael in Manteo, North Carolina.

The purpose of the limited partnership was to acquire, develop and sell real estate in Kitty Hawk, North Carolina. Kitty Hawk is in Dare County. The tract of land (approximately 45 acres) was being "administered" by Peoples Bank and Trust Company, Rocky Mount, North Carolina as trustee for the estate of Pauline Woodard. The property ran from the Atlantic Ocean to the Kitty Hawk Bay. It became known as Kitty Dunes West, Kitty Dunes Village, Kitty Dunes Commercial and Kitty Dunes Annex. The partnership agreement was for ten (10) years.

George W. Neighbors was the *general partner* and Harold B. (Bud) Mays was the *limited partner*. The partnership name was NEIMAY.

Jasper (Jack) Adams was the original partnership accountant. I was told that he followed George W. Neighbors to the Outer Banks in the early 1970s. Sometime during this lawsuit he sold his firm to Johnson, Burgess and Company, Kitty Hawk, North Carolina.

George Neighbors, the *general partner* died July 25, 1983.

Paragraph 19 of the partnership agreement referred to *DISSOLUTION OF PARTNERSHIP. A. THE PARTNERSHIP SHALL BE DISSOLVED UPON THE ADJUDICATION OF INSANITY AND INCOMPETENCY, ADJUDICATION OF BANKRUPTCY, OR DEATH OF THE GENERAL PARTNER.*

In a June 8, 1987 letter from Melinda C. Coffin, Special Agent, Financial Crime Investigations of the North Carolina State Bureau of Investigation to H. P. Williams, Jr., District Attorney of the First Prosecutorial District in the General Court of Justice, she said and I quote, "in order to obtain expert legal guidance in the field of partnership law, I have consulted with Mr. G. Patrick Murphy of the Special Prosecution Division of the Attorney General's Office. Mr. Murphy has also examined the documents previously described. The partnership agreement for Neimay makes specific provision in the event of the death of the **general partner** for the **limited partner** to purchase the assets of the partnership. So far, the Mays have been unable to accomplish this."

At the time of this book going to press, in the year 2004, twenty-one years after the death of George Neighbors, *the estate has not been closed.* There is an issue of THE PARKING LOT in Kitty Dunes West. In addition to that, I, Shirley Mays, agent for the plaintiff, have placed nineteen (19) pages on top of the estate asking to be informed before it is closed.

The following two letters from John B. Neighbors, (known as Jack Neighbors), the executor, to Harold Mays and from his attorney, O. C. Abbott to our attorney, John S. Morrison say it better than I. The letters are dated March 22, 1991 and March 25, 1991.

KITTY DUNES REALTY
P.O. BOX 275
KITTY HAWK, NORTH CAROLINA 27949
TELEPHONE 919/261-2171
COROLLA LIGHT VILLAGE SHOPS
COROLLA, NORTH CAROLINA 27927
TELEPHONE 919/453-3863

THE VACATION PEOPLE

March 22, 1991

Mr. Harold B. Mays
C/O Mr. O. C. Abbott
P. O. Box 69
Elizabeth City, NC 27907

Dear Mr. Mays:

I certainly regret the suit and the expense it cost us, but that is behind us now.

Please find enclosed the 1989 & 1990 Neimay tax returns.

Now that all building lots and contracts have had deeds passed, there is one issue remaining to the final dissolution of Neimay. Tom White strongly recommends we agree on its resolution, so I await your thoughts. On the enclosed Kitty Dunes West plat on Poseidon St. you will see a small lot designated parking lot. I have discussed this at great length with Tom White and subsequently attempted to sell it to adjacent lot owners with no success. My understanding of the original intent was for it to be parking for the subdivision west of the bypass, but this was never recorded anywhere, (The westside lot owners appear to be happy using the parking at the corner of Poseidon and White anyway) precluding that use. The residential zoning and location make it valueless as a commercial parking lot, and it is too small to build on. The property tax department has not recognized this parcel. The outcome is that it becomes common property of the lot owners in Kitty Dunes West, and those lot owners could raise an issue if the property was used to their exclusion. For even the adjacent owners would have limited use rights, and Neimay could only issue a quit-claim deed.

Mr. Mays
Page 2
March 22, 1991

Upon my asking, Tom agreed that the best course is to abandon it and I agree. Please advise.

Sincerely,

John B. Neighbors

JBN/sh

Enclosures

P. S. Carla informed me three weeks ago that we are to be separated and she will seek a divorce (after 17 years).

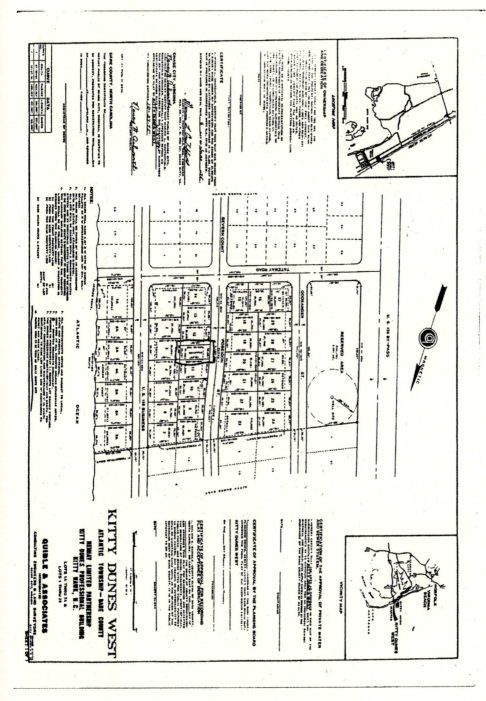

ABBOTT, MULLEN, BRUMSEY & SMALL
ATTORNEYS AT LAW

O.C. ABBOTT
HERBERT T. MULLEN, JR.
WILLIAM BRUMSEY, III
G. ELVIN SMALL, III

101 EAST ELIZABETH STREET
P.O. BOX 69
ELIZABETH CITY, NC 27907
TELEPHONE (919) 335-5442
TELECOPIER 338-2769

P.O. BOX 100
CURRITUCK, NC 27929
TELEPHONE (919) 232-2262
TELECOPIER 232-3056

P.O. BOX 305
KILL DEVIL HILLS, NC 27948
TELEPHONE (919) 441-0404

March 25, 1991

Mr. John S. Morrison
Attorney at Law
P.O. Box 436
Elizabeth City, N.C.   27907-0436

In Re: Mays vs. Neighbors

Dear John:

·I am enclosing an envelope that Jack Neighbors sent to me
addressed to Mr. Harold Mays, without a post office or street
address. He asked me to fill it in, and of course I do not know
the same.

I would appreciate it if you would forward these documents
on to Mr. Mays personally and not to Shirley.

Please note that Jack is sending the 1989 and 1990 Neimay.
tax returns together with a letter personally to Harold Mays.

You would also notice that the postage has already been
placed on the envelope.

With kind personal regards,

Sincerely yours,

ABBOTT, MULLEN, BRUMSEY & SMALL

O. C. Abbott

OCA/ks

Enclosure

cc: John B. Neighbors

Five years later in 1996, it appeared Jack Neighbors was still trying to close the estate without addressing the problems. Shirley Mays was still trying to assume all assets of Neimay so that it could be closed out properly. Jack Neighbors, working with his new attorney, Ron DeVeau of Kill Devil Hills, NC appeared to be putting pressure on the **limited partner** to sign a proposed assignment and release agreement relating to Neimay Limited Partnership.

Shirley Mays' new attorney told Jack Neighbors' new attorney, Ron DeVeau, on March 5, 1996, "my client is suspicious of any resistance against full disclosure. I would suggest that we put this matter to bed as soon as possible before those suspicions take on life."

On <u>January 2, 2004</u>, I visited the new Dare County Judicial Building in Manteo, which houses the office of the Dare County Clerk of Superior Court to review the estate file of George Neighbors. I had not reviewed it for several years. I immediately observed that the "adjustment" documents for a second hidden estate account that I had discovered, and was very concerned about, are not filed together anymore in the folder. In fact, a couple of documents seem to be "rearranged" so as not to highlight the "adjustment." I still have concern after all of these years.

Jack Neighbors had taken action immediately AFTER my new attorney suggested to his new attorney on March 5, 1996 that "we put this matter to bed as soon as possible before those suspicious take on life."

On March 8, 1996, three days after the date of that letter, Jack filed belated annual accountings for 1990, 1991, 1992, 1993, 1994 1995 and one ending March 8, 1996.

The estate is still open as far as I am concerned on January 2, 2004. It is labeled Estate of George Neighbors 83-E-104.

We never signed off on *THE KITTY DUNES WEST PARKING LOT*. The parking lot is valued at $47,500 but no one pays taxes on it. It is exempt for some reason. It is listed in the name of the Kitty Dunes West property owners

– but they are unaware of it. I know this because a clerk in the assessor's office told me on January 2 that she has received several calls from property owners about that particular lot in the last few months of 2003.

I suggested to the new Dare County Clerk of Superior Court, who replaced Betty Mann, that the estate still calls for an investigation by whomever is responsible for criminal activity in estates.

Besides, why should anyone bother to follow the estate rules if everyone doesn't have to?

I, THE AUTHOR OF THIS BOOK, WOULD LIKE TO INFORM JACK NEIGHBORS AND HIS GROUP THAT INDEED, THEY SHOULD HAVE LISTENED TO THAT WISE ATTORNEY OF OURS IN MARCH OF 1996 BECAUSE THOSE SUSPICIONS HAVE DEFINITELY TAKEN ON NEW LIFE – IN THE YEAR 2004.

CHAPTER 3

THE COVER-UP

The following letter is from the Neimay Partnership attorney, Tom White. Tom White was a very prominent real estate attorney from the Manteo Law Firm of Kellogg, White, Evans, Sharp and Michael. I'm showing a few exhibits so you can see the facts for yourself. It appeared Tom wrote this letter out of great concern – for the estate of George Neighbors and Planters National Bank. This letter was not known to the *limited partner* or his agent for a very, very long time. Actually, it was found in some of the executor's discovery at least two years after it was written. The date is August 18, 1983. George died July 25, 1983.

KELLOGG, WHITE, EVANS, SHARP AND MICHAEL
ATTORNEYS AT LAW
P. O. BOX 189
MANTEO, N. C. 27954
TELEPHONE (919) 473-2171

MARTIN KELLOGG, JR.
THOMAS L. WHITE, JR.
CHARLES D. EVANS
STARKEY SHARP
STEVEN D. MICHAEL
ROBERT L. OUTTEN

August 18, 1983

KITTY HAWK OFFICE
P. O. BOX 221
KITTY HAWK, N. C. 27949
TELEPHONE (919) 261-2128

Mr. John B. Neighbors
Executor of the Estate of
   George W. Neighbors
P.O. Box 275
Kitty Hawk, NC 27949

Re: Outstanding Land Sales
     Contracts

Dear Jack:

    This transaction involving Lot 2 of Kitty Dunes Village in which I was
called by Danny Khoury, representing the buyer, to immediately supply a deed
of conveyance is only an example of the bind we find ourselves in, in relation to certain estate matters. The lots in Kitty Dunes Village are all
subject to a deed of trust from which releases have to be obtained from
Peoples Bank and also the Trustees. This usually takes about a week to ten
days turn around time to obtain the four necessary signatures. I have
prepared both the deed and the release deed, transmitting the release deed to
Peoples Bank for execution and return to me, and delivering the deed to Danny
Khoury, who represents the seller, in order that it can be presented to you
for your signature.

    I do not have a contract and so far everything is verbal, nor do I have
a verification from you of the release price except that Danny Khoury gave me
a figure which you had given to him. I am also informed that it is
satisfactory with you that the sum of $5,000.00 out of the sale be held in
escrow in order to cover any liability for estate and inheritance taxes until
such time as the releases from the Internal Revenue Service and the State
Department of Revenue can be obtained. The release price which has to be
paid to Peoples Bank on this particular lot is $4,456.00 by my calculations.

    All of this makes it imperative that I, as soon as possible, receive a
copy of all of the outstanding contracts for any of the partnerships in which
George was the general partner, in order that I can ascertain the terms of
the sale and the sales price. As soon as possible I will also need the
evalutation of all those lots in order that the information can be transmitted to the Internal Revenue Service and the North Carolina Department of
Revenue.

    My best regards,

                              Very truly yours,

                              Thomas L. White, Jr.

TLW:dm
Enclosure

You can readily assume that this panic letter was written shortly after George's death. Little did we know that everyone connected with this Neimay Partnership was or should have been in a state of shock. George had reached out and touched many people. They included lawyers, bankers, accountants, CPAs, and last but not least, the buyers he left hanging with "unrecorded" land contracts.

George personally owed Planters National Bank a lot of money when he died. *They were in one heck of a dilemma.*

It is my hindsight opinion that the only person really in the dark about the terrible state of affairs was his son and executor, Jack Neighbors. George had not shared all of his business dealings with his son. *I am not sure he shared any.* That became obvious very early.

We were a little concerned about our liability but not really as much as we should have been. According to Jack Adams, the creative CPA, we only owed the local bank, Planters National Bank, a small amount of money and we had many assets left to be sold. That was *HIS* story! He should have known because I was told he was on the Board of Directors for Planters National Bank at the time. *George evidently didn't share everything with him either.* It appears that Tom White, the partnership attorney, was the most educated, and his concern seemed to be mostly for the estate and Planters Bank – not the **limited partner**. He was on the Managing Board of Planters National Bank.

During many years of discovery, we found over *28 accounts* connected to George in which Neimay Partnership money had been *commingled* - including an account in Ireland. *Commingle means to mix in or blend – in this case, partnership money with other people's money.*

George's personal banker at Planters did not seem to be concerned that he was check kiting and moving his many Planters bank loans in and out of the accounts. In fact, most of the time the loans were handled automatically by the bank. We found out that George Neighbors had several personal notes at Planters National Bank at the time of his death that had nothing to do with NEIMAY.

According to North Carolina law and the interpretation of the attorney general's office, the partnership should have dissolved *at death*. All the executor had to worry about was *winding up*.

REMEMBER, we had gone to Tom White's office in Manteo shortly after George's death. Tom strongly advised us that we couldn't take over. No advice as to why, just that we couldn't take over. He appeared to be very nervous. Then he wrote the August 18, 1993 letter telling the executor what a bind they were in. This letter was to Jack Neighbors, the executor, who under oath said he knew nothing about his father's business. That revelation later proved to be a *real understatement*.

In retrospect it "appears" that a conspiracy was started at this time, less than a month after George Neighbor's death, to pay off George's personal debts at Planters Bank. It "appears" that *Tom White*, our partnership lawyer, *Jack Adams*, our CPA, *Ray White* and *Chris Payne*, Planters National Bank officials made a united decision that *"somebody"* had to pay George's personal notes. It was going to call for a lot of *creative* banking and *creative* accounting. They were all affiliated one way or another with Planters National Bank. I believe we became their main "somebody."

At this same time, I believe Jack Neighbors, the executor, correctly coined the nickname for them as THE ORIGINAL 4.

CHAPTER 4

PANIC AT PLANTERS BANK

Back in August or September of 1983, approximately two months after George's death, Jack Neighbors, Bud Mays and I went to Planters Bank to meet with Ray White, the President. The executor was still trying to do the legal and honest thing by helping the *limited partner* get the information he needed to take over the partnership. The *limited partner* requested that the Neimay money go into a money market account until the partnership was dissolved. The Mays believed there was quite a bit of money and it should at least be drawing interest. Jack Neighbors agreed.

At that time, the *limited partner* and his wife and the executor were told by Ray White, the President of Planters Bank that the account could be opened but *NOBODY* but the executor could have access to it. That seemed strange, even then, because the *limited partner* was the sole survivor of the Neimay partnership. Ray White acted very uncomfortable that day. We figured it had to be something to do with "freezing" the account. We assumed that no one would be able to pull money out of it without our knowledge. *We assumed wrong.*

After every effort was made to obtain Neimay bank information by both Jack Neighbors and the Mays, the frustrated executor writes a simple little letter of authorization to Ray White, the President of Planters National Bank & Trust Company, in Manteo NC on February 22, 1985 and gives it to Bud and Shirley Mays and their attorney John Morrison to hand-carry to the bank. Jack Neighbors says, in writing, in all innocence to Mr. White to give them everything they want about this partnership because he has nothing to hide.

February 22, 1985

Mr. Ray White, Pres.
Planters National Bank & Trust Co.
Post Office Box 998
Manteo, North Carolina 27954

Re: Neimay Limited Partnership (dissolved).

Dear Ray:

Regarding the Neimay Limited Partnership and all associated bank accounts, historical information of bank accounts, and loans:

Please consider this letter to be my authorization for Mr. Harold B. Mays, Shirley Mays, Warren Ott, and John Morrison, Attorney, to have access to any information contained and copies of anything relating to those aforementioned accounts and loans.

Thank you for your cooperation.

Sincerely,

"Jack Neighbors"   John B. Neighbors, Executor
for the Estate of George W.
Neighbors (deceased)

Pen JACK NEIGHBORS
$40,000

JBN/gb — verified 2/25/85 —

SHIRLEY MAYS 335-0031
                          775-1279

What is it about that letter that was so hard for Ray White, the President of Planters Bank to understand?

The next several letters sing an entirely different tune. It "appears" the executor was immediately enlightened by the President of the bank or *someone* that what he *thought* was Neimay money was *in fact his very own account*. The bank had just made a simple mistake by putting Neimay on the official annual bank report instead of John Neighbors. This is very, very interesting because the account had been opened with a $30,560.78 check from the partnership attorney Tom White. It had been written from the *trust account* of Kellogg, White, Evans, Sharp & Michael and made out *directly* to Planters Bank. The account receiving the check was a money market account opened September 26, 1983 about the time of the panic. It was kept under the name of Neimay for a year and a half until the **limited partner** got his authorization letter dated February 22, 1985. All of a sudden, Jack was told that the account in question was his!

This is the first "correction" of many mistakes that were discovered by us.

LADIES AND GENTLEMEN OF THE JURY

I have a question for you right in the early stages of this case. Do you or anybody you know have over $30,000 in a bank account that you are unaware of?

It appears Jack Neighbors did.

SHIRLEY MAYS

P O BOX 275
KITTY HAWK, NORTH CAROLINA
27949
TELEPHONE 919/261-2171

February 25, 1985

Mr. Ray White
Mr. Wilson Shearin
Planters National Bank & Trust Co.
Post Office Box 998
Manteo, North Carolina 27954

Gentlemen:

Concerning a letter of last week in which I requested that you release information on Neimay to Mrs. Shirley Mays and others. A Planters National Bank statement, copy enclosed, identified three accounts as Neimay. Account No. 005-090-3 is a Neimay account; please release that information. The following two accounts are not Neimay accounts, and under no conditions is any information about those accounts to be released. They are No. 319-565-1 and 356-04-8.

The combined tax statement, which I have enclosed, is obviously completely wrong and I would appreciate that being broken down into separate statements - one for Neimay and one for my personal accounts. Neimay tax ID# 56-1049350 - please notify IPS of correct copy
Thank you very much.

Sincerely,

John B. Neighbors

JBN/gb

Enclosures

cc: Mrs. Shirley L. Mays
     John S. Morrison, Esq.

MEMORANDUM

TO: Vernell Logan

FROM: Wilson Shearin

DATE: February 27, 1985

SUBJECT: NEIMAY Limited

The attached tax statement indicates two accounts under the name of NEIMAY Limited that should be listed to John B. Neighbors' social security number 225-70-2763. Please revise this document to reflect the Money Market account number 319-565-1 and savings account number 35604-8 in the name of Mr. Neighbors. The NEIMAY Tax ID number is 56-1099350.

Please contact me if you have any questions regarding this matter.

Thank you.

Wilson Shearin

WS/dw

February 25, 1985

Planters
Bank

Mr. John Morrison
Attorney at Law
P. O. Box 384
Elizabeth City, N. C, 27909

Re: NEIMAY Limited

Dear Mr. Morrison:

In researching your recent request, I find that account #319-565-1 and account #35604-8 are not listed under NEIMAY Limited. I will be unable to provide any copies of statements regarding these two accounts.

Please contact me if you have any questions, or if I can be of any further assistance.

Sincerely,

Wilson Shearin
Assistant Vice President

WS/dw
cc: John B. Neighbors

JENNETTE, MORRISON, AUSTIN & HALSTEAD
ATTORNEYS AT LAW
P. O. BOX 384
300 E. CHURCH STREET
ELIZABETH CITY, N.C. 27909

J. W. JENNETTE (Retired)
JOHN S. MORRISON
C. GLENN AUSTIN
JOHN W. HALSTEAD, JR.

919 335-5413

February 25, 1985

Mr. Jack Neighbors
Kitty Dunes Realty
P. O. Box 275
Kitty Hawk, N. C. 27949

Re: Dissolution of Neimay Partnership

Dear Jack:

I was very distressed to learn today from Shirley that evidently you are now contending that Money Market Investment Account No. 319-565-1 and Savings Account No. 35604-8 at Planters Bank in Manteo were not in fact Neimay accounts but were your personal accounts.

I distinctly recall asking you this on last Friday, and you advised me at that time that they were Neimay accounts and contained Neimay money. Furthermore, it appears that you are asking Planters Bank not to honor our request for an examination of these records, despite the fact that you had given us a letter of authority to that end.

As you are aware, there are a great many unanswered questions concerning the operation of the partnership and the cash flow. Your refusal to allow us to examine these documents, which are clearly labeled Neimay accounts, causes additional confusion in consternation. I do not wish to become involved in litigation but should that become necessary, we will clearly be allowed to examine these records. Also, I am still confused as to what you meant about "reading between the lines" on the promissory note that is signed in your father's name, but does not appear to be in his handwriting.

Please respond immediately as to whether or not we are going to be able to examine these records, whether you intend to interfere in allowing us to look at the promissory notes signed by the partnership and when you will provide the settlement sheets we requested, which you have admitted are in your files under the real estate company. If I do not hear from you, or your counsel, should you so elect, by March 4, 1985, I will assume that you wish to withhold this information.

Mr. Jack Neighbors
February 25, 1985
Page ·2

My clients do not mean to pry into your private affairs, and if these Neimay accounts are in fact your own money, it will clearly be apparent from the transaction in and out, and of course they will make no claim. But under the unusual circumstance of you maintaining your personal money under two Neimay accounts, I think they are certainly entitled to see where the money came from and where it went.

Please give this your most prompt attention in order that matters do not deteriorate further.

Sincerely,

JENNETTE, MORRISON, AUSTIN & HALSTEAD

John S. Morrison

ss

cc Shirley Mays

KITTY DUNES REALTY
P O BOX 275
KITTY HAWK, NORTH CAROLINA
27949
TELEPHONE 919/261-2171

FEB. 28 1985

February 26, 19

John S. Morrison, Esq.
Jennette, Morrison,
Austin & Halstead
PO Box 384
Elizabeth City, NC 27909

Re: Neimay Limited Partnership

Dear John:

Regarding a great number of the financial questions in the Neimay audit; Jack Adams, CPA, cans supply answers to almost all of them from his work files and records and his professional knowledge of Neimay. For your convenience, he is holding open the dates of March 6, 7, and 8 so that you may conveniently schedule an appointment with him to review these matters and find a resolution to them. Mr. Adams would appreciate it if it would be possible for you to solidify this schedule some time this week. Thank you for your attention to this. I am confident that this will relieve a great majority of questions.

Additionally, I am enclosing a brief description of a rather unpleasant situation which occurred this afternoon simply for your recognizance.

Sincerely,

John B. Neighbors

JBN/gb

Enclosure

cc: Mrs. Shirley Mays

February 26, 19

2:30 - 2:45 F

From: John B. Neighbors

At my request, Mrs. Shirley Mays came into my offices(with Mr.
Warren Ott). I gave her a copy of the Planters National Bank &
Trust Company statement, a letter from Planters and my letter to
Planters regarding bank accounts.

Additionally, I gave her the checks from Resh & Egli and payment
card that we had received in the mail a few days ago. (Mrs. Egli said
it had been mailed on 2/15/85.) Mrs. Mays took the payment card and chec
then handed the checks back to me, refusing to accept them. She said th
reason for this was that the checks were made out to "Neimay". I offered
to endorse them over to her, but she refused.

I then sent them back to Resh & Egli with instructions to make them
payable to Shirley Mays. I phoned this information to Mr. Resh and Mr.
Egli as well.

P. S.: I am assembling the documents Mrs. Mays requested for the
        audit, but I do have a very tight schedule, and do <u>not</u> have
        time for this kind of childishness.

KITTY DUNES REALTY
P O BOX 275
KITTY HAWK, NORTH CAROLINA
27949
TELEPHONE 919/261-2171

For Your Information - March 4, 1985

MAR. 0 1 1985

February 27, 19

John S. Morrison, Esq.
Jennette, Morrison;
Austin & Halstead
Post Office Box 384
Elizabeth City, NC 27909

Re: Neimay Limited Partnership

Dear John:

In reply to your letter of February 25, 1985, I am certainly most
distressed at the tone of your letter After discussing this matter
and discovering the truth about these bank accounts from Mr. Wilson
Shearin at Planters Bank in Manteo, he will be supplying you with a
letter that authenticates the following facts, of which I was obviously
rather confused about the other day.

First, Account #005-090-3 is the Neimay Money Market account. The
other two accounts listed on the combined tax statement are in no way,
shape or form or anything else related to Neimay. Planters Bank was
totally wrong in listing those on a Neimay tax statement. They are
supplying corrected tax statements and a letter to back up the fact
that they were totally wrong in doing so. Those other two accounts
are my personal accounts and are not related to Neimay in any way
shape or form. As I mentioned, I was mistaken the other day because
that was over a year ago at a confusing time, but I can assure you that
no Neimay money ever entered those accounts, in any case.

Regarding the unanswered financial questions, my call to your office
the other day, and I obviously now feel that this must be in writing, you
will find that probably all, at least most if not all, financial questions
will be answered by Jack Adams, who has a much more thorough knowledge
of Neimay's financial status than I do. Mr. Adams has retained three
open days on his calendar to accommodate all of you, the 6-7-8th of March.
I do not have the answers, Mr. Adams does. My personal accounts will provide no insight whatsoever into anything relating to Neimay. That is why
access is not required since the questions will be answered.

With regard to the closing statements, settlement sheets and such,
we are gathering those together. My secretary has been working on this
very diligently and thoroughly. I believe we will have them all together
by the time of our meeting with Mr. Adams next week.

Your letter implied that I intended to interfere in your examination
of promissory notes signed by the partnership. I do not know where that
impression came from, because that is just ridiculous. There will be no

interference whatsoever in any Neimay affairs, and certainly not with regard to any promissory notes.

Your next to the last paragraph refers to your clients prying into my personal affairs. I can assure you that they will not get into my personal affairs. There will be no questions remaining, I believe, after our conference with Mr. Adams. I do not have need of using an attorney, and I feel perfectly comfortable dealing directly with you. However, if any information regarding my personal accounts is released to Mr. and Mrs. Mays and/or Mr. Ott, I will immediately turn the entire matter over to Tom White, as this would be an invasion of my privacy.

Again, all the information you need and have requested will be supplied by Planters Bank, Jack Adams, or myself.

Sincerely,

John B. Neighbors

JBN/gb

You must remember – most of this information had to be pieced together years later because the discovery was dragged out for over seven years. Some Planters National Bank officials were adamant about not giving up any of their *secrets*. Unfortunately, that put the **limited partner** past all statutes of limitation. The **limited partner's** attorney, John Morrison, always told us *not to worry about the statutes* – they won't run out – right up to the time of trial. We believed our attorney.

LADIES AND GENTLEMEN OF THE JURY

Let us just review a few facts. We have a partnership attorney, Tom White, telling the executor that they are in a bind. You have an executor, Jack Neighbors, trying real hard to be honest. You have an executor trying to cooperate with the **limited partner** but you have the president of the local bank confusing him.

The executor thought *he* was broke and the banker is telling him that he has lots of money.

Confusing -----------and interesting, isn't it?

Then all of a sudden, the executor tells John Morrison that he is upset with **the limited partner** and he is thinking about suing.

Subtle he's not.

I think the Original 4 have a problem on their hands with their new leader if they expect him to play it cool!

You know what, ladies and gentlemen of the jury. I don't care who is confusing the executor. He personally just threw the first stone at us.

SHIRLEY MAYS

KITTY DUNES REALTY
P O BOX 275
KITTY HAWK, NORTH CAROLINA
27949
TELEPHONE 919/261-2171

March 1, 1985

John S. Morrison, Esq.
Mr. Harold B. Mays
Mrs. Shirley Mays
Jennette, Morrison,
Austin & Halstead
Post Office Box 384
Elizabeth City, NC 27909

Re: Neimay Limited Partnership

Gentlemen and Shirley:

Your letters of late have demanded answers to numerous questions you have regarding Neimay finances. The meeting the other day was for me a surprise in that I had requested the meeting for the purpose of delivering the payment check, which you had accepted at that time. I was not prepared to meet with the three of you, as you could see, in order to discuss a series of questions for which I have no answers personally. The remainder of your questions, as I have told Mr. Morrison's office several times this week, will probably all be able to be answered by Mr. Jack Adams, CPA, who did the Neimay tax returns, as near as I can tell, from the time of Neimay's inception. I have told you that I do not have an answer to a number of these questions because I was not involved in the Neimay partnership until after my father's death. As of today, Friday, March 1, 1985 at 11:30 a.m., neither the Mays nor Mr. Morrison have bothered to make an appointment with Jack Adams, who is maintaining three open days on his calendar next week - Wednesday, Thursday or Friday the 6th, 7th or 8th of March - for you to schedule a meeting at your convenience. The purpose of this appointment if for you to obtain answers to your questions with the person who can supply them.

Again, I am offering you the answers through Mr. Adams, the CPA for Neimay. If it is your choice not to accept the information, then there is nothing more I can do for you and we will probably have to spend thousands of dollars in litigation. I see no need for that. It is not my intent to do that; but, only you can make appointments for yourselves with this gentleman who does have the answers to your questions.

Thank you for your consideration of these suggestions and comments.

Sincerely,

John B. Neighbors

JBN/gb
Original to J. Morrison
Copies to Mr. and Mrs. Mays

CHAPTER 5

THE INFAMOUS $40,000 *"PERSONAL"* NOTE

This personal bank note of the ***general partner*** was a big issue to us - and should be to all of you who deal with a bank. I am going to elaborate on it because if you are ever lucky or unlucky enough to be a ***limited partner*** in a real estate deal on the Outer Banks, I want you to be aware of how very creative bank officials can become – when *anyone* owes them money. At the time of this particular creativity, it was Planters National Bank. Centura inherited or should have inherited all of their problems at the time of merger with Planters and Peoples. They are now RBC Centura Bank.

It may be of interest for you to know that in the world of real estate, ***commingle*** *means the illegal practice by a real estate broker of maintaining personal or business funds in the same account with trust funds held by others.*

1. George Neighbors died July 25, 1983. The $40,000 credit application in question is dated *or* backdated June 23, 1983. You will notice it is a "personal" note for George Neighbors but payment is to come from Neimay funds? The applicant was "not present" (maybe departed) and the note is not signed. The repayment source involves a "fisherman" and Neimay money. Chris Payne, Planters Bank official is the loan officer.

    Is this unsigned credit application acceptable to the FDIC? It is *not acceptable* to the ***limited partner***.

SHIRLEY MAYS

CORPORATION ☐ PARTNERSHIP ☐
PROPRIETORSHIP ☐ INDIVIDUAL ☑

002-930-0
NEIMAY 4D PNSHP
1-430

PNB Reviewed 4-30-84

APPLICATION FOR CREDIT

LOAN OFFICER: Payne
BRANCH: Manteo
DATE: 6-23-83

IMPORTANT: Read these directions before completing this Application.

☐ If you are applying for individual credit in your own name and are relying on your own income or assets and not the income or assets of another person as the basis for repayment of the credit requested, complete only Section 1.
☑ If you are applying for joint credit with another person, complete all Sections providing information in Section 2 about the joint applicant.
☐ If you are applying for individual credit, but are relying on income from alimony, child support or separate maintenance or on the income or assets of another person as a basis for repayment of the credit requested, complete all Sections, providing information in Section 2 about the person on whose alimony, support, or maintenance payments or income or assets you are relying.
☐ If this application relates to your guaranty of the indebtedness of other person(s), firm(s) or corporation(s), complete Section 1.

SECTION 1: Applicant Information

DO NOT COMPLETE IF THIS APPLICATION IS FOR INDIVIDUAL, CR
☐ MARRIED ☐ UNMARRIED ☐ SEPARATED

NAME: George W. Neighbors
ADDRESS: Box 275, Kitty Hawk, N.C.
FORMER ADDRESS:

BIRTHDATE | PHONE | SOCIAL SECURITY NO.
HOW LONG | ☐ OWN ☐ RENT | REAL PROPERTY VALUE $
HOW LONG | NO. DEPENDENTS

EMPLOYER | ADDRESS | HOW LONG
POSITION OR OCCUPATION | HOW LONG | FORMER EMPLOYER | HOW LONG

*ALIMONY, CHILD SUPPORT OR SEPARATE MAINTENANCE INCOME NEED NOT BE REVEALED IF YOU DO NOT WISH TO HAVE IT CONSIDERED AS A BASIS FOR REPAYING THIS OBLIGATION.

PRESENT ANNUAL INCOME | SOURCE | *OTHER INCOME | *SOURCE
NEAREST RELATIVE NOT LIVING WITH APPLICANT | ADDRESS
NAMES AND AGES OF PRINCIPALS OR PARTNERS IF BUSINESS APPLICANT

PRINCIPAL BANK(S): PNB (see reverse)
DDA AVG. BAL. $ 176,900 SAVINGS BAL. $
LOANS: COMM $ 26,000 MTG $ 13,7
INSTALL. $ CHK. CR. $ MC $

THE PROCEEDS OF THIS LOAN ARE TO BE USED FOR THE FOLLOWING PURPOSE:
☐ PERSONAL ☑ BUSINESS ☐ AGRICULTURAL

CREDIT REFERENCES | PAYMENTS | BALANCE

REQUESTED CREDIT: $40,000
REPAYMENT AGREEMENT (BE SPECIFIC): ADAM 9-15-83
RATE: P+1

PURPOSE (BE SPECIFIC): Pay balance of 1st mortgage + all other debts on Neimay property
SOURCE OF FUNDS FOR REPAYMENT: $41,900 Note all due Billy Beasley on 9-10-83

ENDORSEMENT OR COLLATERAL: Etux
APPRAISED VALUE
MARGIN (%)

SECTION 2: Other Applicant
*IF OTHER APPLICANT IS CONTRACTUALLY LIABLE, COMPLETE THE FOLLOWING SECTION. IF YOU ARE RELYING ON SPOUSE'S INCOME, OR HAVE PREVIOUSLY DISCLOSED THAT YOU ARE RELYING ON ALIMONY, CHILD SUPPORT OR MAINTENANCE PAYMENTS FROM A SPOUSE OR FORMER SPOUSE AS THE BASIS FOR REPAYMENT ON THIS ACCOUNT, COMPLETE THE FOLLOWING SECTION.

PRESENT OUTSTANDING 26,000 L/S NEW CREDIT
TOTAL CREDIT APPROVED 13,789 O/S 40,000
COMMENTS ON REVERSE $ 79,789

NAME OF OTHER APPLICANT | AGE | CENSUS TRACT NO
ADDRESS
EMPLOYER | POSITION | ANNUAL INCOME
HOW LONG ☐ YRS ☐ MOS | PREVIOUS EMPLOYER
PHONE NUMBER | *OTHER INCOME (SOURCE) | AMOUNT (ANNUAL)
CREDIT REFERENCES | PAYMENTS | BALANCE

If Checked here the collateral involved is being acquired with the proceeds of the loan here to be applied for and Bank may disburse proceeds directly to Seller of said collateral. The collateral involved is bought or used primarily for
☐ Personal, family or household purposes
☐ farming operations use
☐ business use

DISCLOSURE AND WARRANTY
DISCLOSURE An Investigative Consumer Report including information as to your character, general reputation, personal characteristics and mode of living whichever are applicable may be made in connection with your credit request. Within a reasonable time you have a right to make a written request and to receive a complete and accurate disclosure of the nature and scope of any such investigation made or requested.
The undersigned warrants the information furnished herein, for the purpose of obtaining credit to be true and complete and acknowledges receipt of the foregoing DISCLOSURE.

Not present

APPLICANT
APPLICANT

40

2. The "purported" repayment note of this personal note of George Neighbors is dated the same date June 23, 1983 and also is unsigned. The executor told me that Adams, our CPA originated the note.

    Wouldn't you question the legality of all of these unsigned notes if you were the *limited partner?*

Exhibit 3

June 23, 1983
(Date)

FOR VALUE RECEIVED, ___Neimay Limited Partnership___

promises to pay to the order of ___George W. Neighbors and Dorothy T. Neighbors___

the principal sum of $___40,000.00___ due and payable

___September 15, 1983___

WITH INTEREST THEREON at the rate of (13½) per cent per annum on

the unpaid principal balance from date until paid, payable concurrently

with and in addition to the principal payment.

IN TESTIMONY WHEREOF the said ___Neimay Limited Partnership___

has caused this instrument to be executed in ___its___ name.

_____
George W. Neighbors,
General Partner

Borrowed from Planters National Bank (Ray White) Loaned to Neimay

3. The cashiers check, clearly "cut" for $4000 was made out to Neimay on the very same day, June 23, 1983. But the deposit slip shows $40,000 deposited into the Neimay account on June 23, 1983. Isn't that a difference of $36,000? Where did the $36,000 come from? Which is correct - $4000 or $40,000? How does that affect the bank books? Is that just sloppy bookkeeping?

    If you were the *limited partner,* wouldn't you question this?

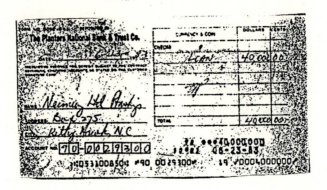

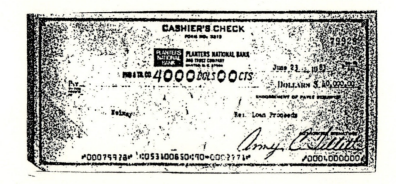

4. This is a Planters Bank Commercial Loan Account History Ledger involving this creative transaction. It is clearly a personal note for George Neighbors but all the payments are made *AFTER* death. Four of them represent Neimay closings – all performed without the ***limited partner's*** knowledge – with payments coming from the trust account of Tom White's law firm. This is at the same time the ***limited partner*** is desperately trying to get information.

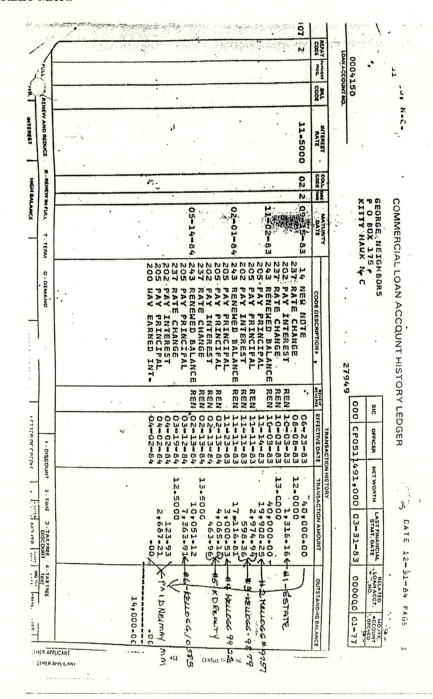

5. This is a chart (by the plaintiff's agent) with the figures taken
    from Jack Adams "unaudited" audit. It is very, very creative
    accounting and shows how the personal note was paid off.
    These closings of properties were without the knowledge of
    the *limited partner*. It appears that the partnership attorney, the
    CPA and the bankers were acting on behalf of the estate and
    the bank to pay off this personal note. One of the stubs says,
    "Orig. 4 OK."

PERSONAL NOTE OF GEORGE NEIGHBORS
$40,000 – NOTE #78907 – DATED 6-23-83

PAYMENT HISTORY
AND
POSTING BY JACK ADAMS, CPA

Trans/Date	Prin/Int	Source/Explanation	1985 Posting/Adams
#1-10-3-83	$1,316.16 Int.	Pd. by Estate #316-156-0 Ck. 008 dtd 10-3-83 (Stub $2788.46)	none
#2 - 11-14-83	$19,908.25 P	Pd. from Settlement Sheet of Tom White (Beasley) w/Kellogg ck. #9757 to PNB	($19,908.25) Loan to GWN
#3- 11-11-83	$ 2,974.94 P 598.36 Int	Pd. from Settlement Sheet of Tom White (Olds) w/ Kellogg ck. #9879 to PNB	$1,908.49 Interest ($1,654.81) Loan to GWN
#4 - 11-23-83	$3,000.53 P	Pd. from Settlement Sheet of Tom White (Ryder) w/Kellogg ck. #9922 to PNB	($3,000.53) Loan to GWN
#5- 2-13-84	$4,065.16 P 463.96 Int	Pd. by K.D.Realty ck.#603 **stub says "orig. 4 o.k."**	($4,065.16) Loan to GWN 463.96 Interest
#6 - 3-12-84	$7,363.91 P	Pd. by Settlement Sheet of Tom White (Barger) w/Kellogg ck. #10583	($7,239.98) Loan to GWN $123.93 Interest
#7 - 4-2-84	$2,687.21 P 123.93 Int	Pd. from Neimay MM Acct. Ck. #004 for $2811.14	Loan to GWN

*It is not OK with the **limited partner**.*

HOW CAN THE BUYERS HAVE CLEAR TITLES IF THE *LIMITED PARTNER* DIDN'T SIGN THE DEEDS AND WHO INSURED THEM?

I need to give you a little background on Tom White, the Neimay Partnership attorney. What better source than his own words. The following facts are taken directly from his deposition on September 12, 1986 at 10:00 a.m. in Kitty Hawk, NC. Present were: John Morrison, Esquire, Counsel for the Plaintiff; O. C. Abbott, Esquire, Counsel for the Defendant; Shirley Mays, Agent for the Plaintiff; Jack Neighbors and Peggy Berry, the Reporter. He stipulates:

- that he is an attorney from the University of North Carolina Law School
- that he has been licensed since September 1970
- that his practice is about seventy-five percent real estate and real estate litigation
- that he consulted very little with John Neighbors with regard to winding up the partnership because he was aware that there was disagreement between the Mays and Jack Neighbors and he felt he might be in a conflicting situation
- that in regards to why the ninety-day inventory and annual inventory had been so late, he was aware that Jack Adams was handling that and he had advised Jack Neighbors of timely notice and the power the Clerk of Court had with relation to requiring those and what the clerk could do if not filed on time.
- that in response to a question asked since George Neighbors' death or since July 25, 1983; have you made any payments from Neimay proceeds, from loans you closed or any other Neimay money you may have had control of; have you made payments to any bank and the loan was not designated Neimay. The answer was "No, I don't believe I have. I don't recall that I have."
- that on page 11 of his deposition he stated that he had been

on the local board of managers for Planters for five or six years.

On the same day, September 12, 1986 with the same people in attendance, Chris Payne stipulated in his deposition:

- that he was a Vice-President of Planters National Bank in Manteo, NC
- that he had been the loan officer for the $40,000 loan
- that if anything happened to George, the bank *would look to his estate* for the payment of that note

Chris Payne also *repeated under oath* the second day of the Neimay trial that Planters Bank considered the $40,000 note to be a personal responsibility of the deceased George Neighbors.

With these facts in mind, let me try to illustrate to you how very "creative" these prominent well known gentlemen were in "disposing" of this infamous $40,000 Planters National Bank *personal* note of the deceased *general partner* George Neighbors *WHILE USING NEIMAY PARTNERSHIP MONEY* – without the knowledge of the **limited partner.**

- A Planters Bank official *automatically*, with a transfer slip, took $40,233.75 out of the main Neimay account saying it was put in there in error in July.

  What's a mistake about putting Neimay money into a Neimay account?

  The slip stated that it went in by mistake in July. It was clearly dated in September and deposited in September. It was taken out in October – saying it was put in by mistake. Then it was automatically transferred into the *Kitty Dunes Realty Escrow account* where Jack Neighbors was able to write a check for the very same amount to the Kellogg firm so they could deposit it in their *trust* account.

  It is <u>EXACTLY</u> the same amount $40,233.75 recorded on a

settlement statement by Tom White in an improper closing
with Billy Beasley, a fisherman, on October 17, 1983 –
almost three months after the death of the **general partner.**
That closing represents the #2 payment on the infamous
$40,000 note. The settlement statements were "lost"
for years. When discovered, someone had made several
changes on Tom White's settlement statements.

These were clearly Neimay funds – *beyond a reasonable
doubt.*

- Tom White, at this time, without the knowledge or
  permission of the **limited partner**, closed four Neimay
  land transactions. *This was during the time that he was
  advising the Mays that they could not take over the
  partnership.* He retained $5000 out of each Neimay
  closing to pay the inheritance taxes arising from the estate
  of George Neighbors. He paid the release amounts to
  People's Bank on the purchase money note. He *always*
  paid himself for preparation of deed, release deed, retaining
  funds for release from State and U. S. Inheritance taxes,
  disbursement and closing. And he always managed to get
  enough money to pay Planters Bank until that infamous
  $40,000 personal note was paid off for George. *If this was
  proper, why didn't he explain this to **the limited partner**
  who was trying to take over?*

  *And he said, under oath, he didn't think he did that. I can
  prove that he did – beyond a reasonable doubt.*

- These closings were started immediately after Tom's August
  18, 1983 letter when he notified the executor, in writing, that
  "they" were in a real bind. These closings occurred between
  October 3, 1983 and April 2, 1984 in the same time frame
  that the **limited partner** was trying to get information so he
  could take over the partnership.

The documentation will prove this – beyond a reasonable doubt.

- There were seven payments made on this infamous $40,000 personal note. Four were paid directly to Planters Bank with trust checks from Tom White involving money *taken out of Neimay closings.* One was from the "reported" estate account. One was from the first Neimay money market account. One was from the Kitty Dunes Realty escrow account – stub says "Orig 4 OK."

It is worthy to note at this time, that the posting performed by Jack Adams, CPA, on this infamous $40,000 note was so "creative" that it was almost impossible to connect it to the note in question. The principal and interest amounts were changed and put under incorrect columns.

*The court ordered audit that Adams had to furnish the **limited partner** would prove this – beyond a reasonable doubt.*

REMEMBER

THIS IS AN ACCOUNTING LAWSUIT

Also remember, the discovery was dragged out from 1983 to 1991 because we found it very difficult to get any settlement statements or other discovery from the lawyers, bankers, accountants or the executor.

I would like to present to you, the jury, a few questions about that infamous $40,000 note and the creative way it was paid off. This should be of interest to bankers, law students, accounting students, real estate agents, real estate buyers and *limited partners* everywhere who just might innocently get involved with a real estate scam.

- Was it legal for Tom White to withhold partnership monies out of Neimay closings (after death) without the permission of the *limited partner* in order to pay the deceased *general*

partner's Federal and State Inheritance taxes?

- Should Tom White's fiduciary responsibility, at that time, be to the ***limited partner,*** the deceased ***general partner's*** estate or the bank?

- How did Tom White close those Neimay properties without the ***limited partner's*** permission when by NC law, the partnership was supposed to automatically dissolve at the death of the ***general partner***?

- Was it legal for Tom White to send Neimay money directly to Planters Bank from his trust account to be applied on a personal note of the deceased ***general partner*** – without the permission of the ***limited partner?***

- How did Tom White deliver clear titles and get title insurance for these properties when the ***limited partner*** was not aware of the closings and definitely did not sign the deeds?

- Did Jack Neighbors, the executor, act as ***general partner*** improperly even though the partnership was supposed to be dissolved?

- If the CPA was so sure this infamous note was a responsibility of Neimay, why did he feel compelled to change the correct principal and interest amounts and put them under incorrect columns?

- Is it a crime to deliberately falsify settlement statements while blocking the trail of value?

Let me leave you with this *one very important* question. The executor himself paid one of the payments on this personal $40,000 note out of the Kitty Dunes Realty Escrow account and he put a notation on his check, which said "*O.K. ed by the Orig 4 for GWN personal note.*" *How is this escrow transaction justified with the Real Estate Commission? Wouldn't this be identified as commingling?*

LADIES AND GENTLEMEN OF THE JURY

WHO ARE THE ORIGINAL 4 AND WHAT IS THEIR GAME?

CHAPTER 6

THE NEIMAY LAWSUIT

By March 20, 1985, we had made every effort possible to try to gather information about the Neimay Partnership.

- The bankers were not responding to the *limited partner's* request for information about Neimay loans.

- The partnership lawyer couldn't seem to find his settlement statements or any other records pertaining to these questionable closings.

- The partnership accountant's "unaudited" audit was *extremely* questionable.

- The EXECUTOR was *definitely* getting hostile.

WHAT CHOICE IS THERE BUT A LAWSUIT?

The *limited partner* appointed me, his wife, as his agent. I suggested to John Morrison, our attorney, that we sue the executor and the Original 4. He informed us that it would be difficult to prove a conspiracy so the best thing would be to sue the executor. I asked him to request a jury but he said a jury wouldn't understand an accounting lawsuit. He said we could always request one later.

So on March 20, 1985, a formal notice of claim was given to John B. Neighbors, Executor of the Estate of George Neighbors against the Estate of George Neighbors.

On March 22, 1985, formal notices were given to the President of Planters National Bank in Rocky Mount, North Carolina and to the Trust

SHIRLEY MAYS

Officer for Peoples Bank and Trust Company in Rocky Mount, North Carolina that Shirley Mays, the plaintiff's agent was authorized to examine the books and records of the Neimay partnership for purposes of facilitating an accounting.

By the time of trial in 1991, these two popular banks had merged into one big institution – Centura Bank.

The filing of this case was definitely the beginning of a mockery of justice within the judicial system of my home state of North Carolina. We had no idea what we were about to experience.

- I believed in the constitutional right of a fair and speedy trial.

- I believed that when a judge called for discovery, it was to be produced.

- I believed that banks (Federal and State) were basically honest institutions and existed to protect our hard earned monies.

- I believed that lawyers had a fiduciary responsibility to their clients.

- I believed that executors of estates had a very serious fiduciary responsibility to all of the parties involved in the estate.

- I believed that the clerk of court was there to see that the estates were handled properly.

- I believed that district attorneys were elected to represent the people and enforce the law.

SO MUCH FOR BELIEF IN THE JUDICIAL SYSTEM

I am presenting this alleged conspiracy to you as simply as possible *because it could happen to you.*

I am writing this book to expose this scam because the system failed us. I think the timing is good because most of the public is following the security frauds presently being exposed on Wall Street by Eliot Spitzer, the New York Attorney General. He's having a difficult time exposing all of the accounting frauds. As the public knows, it is almost impossible to expose this type of fraud in the courts because it's a numbers game. The corporate criminals desperately want you to believe it is *"just sloppy bookkeeping"* when it is mostly falsified records. Believe me, we tried very hard!

Always keep in mind throughout this book that this is an accounting lawsuit.

It is a **Limited Partnership**.

There was one *general partner* and one *limited partner.*

It was our first experience with a real estate partnership of any kind. We went into it with a very positive attitude and a lot of trust. We were satisfied we had a good partnership agreement. *The **general partner** just did not follow the agreement.* If he had not died before the partnership ended in 1985, *we* could have ended up in quite a bind *instead* of the estate. We could have lost our investment and inherited a pile of lawsuits from all of the unrecorded land deals.

LADIES AND GENTLEMEN OF THE JURY

Please be aware that I have volumes and volumes of documentation accumulated over a period of 20 years that will *NOT* be in *THIS* book. Many other attorneys were involved in these shady closings of our Neimay assets. I wonder if they were informed that they needed the signatures of the **surviving limited partner** in order to have a clear deed. There are at least sixteen other deeds out there in Dare County, which were closed after the death of George Neighbors and *NOT SIGNED* by the surviving **limited partner**. *You may have one of them.* Remember, Tom White, who is by his own definition, an expert real estate attorney, was closing these properties behind the scenes without our knowledge and without the signature of the **limited partner.**

RBC Centura should check for accuracy all of their deeds of trust and the titles of the properties on which they are relying. On October 26, 1987, a letter was sent from E. Crouse Gray, Jr. of the Kellogg, *White,* Evans and *Gray* firm to our attorney John Morrison which said, "In order to clear the title to the property, the title insurance company has requested that the deed from Neimay Limited Partnership be both from John B. Neighbors, as Executor of the Estate of George W. Neighbors, and from Mr. Harold Mays, the other partner."

HOW DID TOM WHITE GET TITLE INSURANCE ON THESE PROPERTIES? WHO OWNS THE TITLE COMPANIES? EVEN THE JUDGE WANTED TO KNOW THAT! THE TESTIMONY ON THAT WAS NOT CLEAR.

On July 5, 1985, Jack Neighbors asked the Dare County Clerk of Superior Court, Betty Mann, for a thirty-day extension. Quote, "The reason for this request is the extreme difficulty in finding an attorney who has not either represented the partnership involved in the suit or discussed the case with the plaintiff or his associate, or previously represented the plaintiff or his associates. I have looked in Dare, Currituck and Pasquotank and will apparently have to go outside this area."

Jack's father had reached out and touched a lot of people! They *should* be concerned about conflicts of interest.

The only attorney he found who would even consider taking this high exposure case was a gentleman from Elizabeth City, North Carolina – my hometown. He was a family friend, who decided, in his late forties to go to law school. I had heard he only took ambulance or emergency cases. By this time, I am sure it was becoming an emergency case for Jack Neighbors. The attorney's name is O. C. Abbott.

On July 8, 1985, O. C. Abbott, on behalf of Jack Neighbors, filed a Motion for Extension of Time. This was to be the first of many motions. His reason was that the attorney had not had time to prepare for filing responsive pleadings. On August 9, 1985, Mr. Abbott filed a Motion that simply said

John B. Neighbors is *NOT* a necessary or proper party in this action. That he has had no connection with the Neimay Limited Partnership other than as executor of the estate of George Neighbors.

I BELIEVE THAT PLAINLY SAYS THAT JOHN NEIGHBORS HAS NO CONNECTION WITH NEIMAY. THAT MEANS HE HAS NO AUTHORITY TO MAKE NEIMAY DECISIONS.

REMEMBER, behind the scenes during this crucial time, Tom White and others were closing Neimay land deals without the knowledge or permission of the **limited partner**. They appeared desperate to pay off George's personal debts at Planters Bank. If Jack had NO connection with the Neimay Limited Partnership, as his new attorney legally stated, then surely he was informed by Tom White, the partnership attorney, not to make any decisions concerning Neimay assets.

In February of 1986, Tom White wrote Jack Neighbors and informed him they were trying to wrap up old firm accounts as a result of the "*reorganization*" of their law firm. During their reorganization, which we were not aware of, we were trying to get settlement statements from Tom White. It appears there were not many settlement statements available *because of the manner in which they were closed? Not very much paperwork involved?* Later we found out that his billings for these particular closings were impossible to track because sometimes he grouped them together on one settlement statement – sometimes they were on the wrong settlement statement – and sometimes it was just a cash check that I happened to find with a notation on it. The misleading information appeared to be intentional. You must keep reminding yourself that Tom White is an EXPERT real estate attorney by his own admission.

Right after this reorganization of the Kellogg firm, Mr. Abbott filed a Response to Motion to Compel that said John Neighbors had searched the records of Neimay in an effort to produce all documents requested. That everything in his possession had been produced. That all closing attorneys had been requested to furnish copies of closing documents but *none of the documents, subject to the Motion to Compel*, had been found as of that date. That the failure to produce had not been the fault of John B. Neighbors,

Executor, but was due to the inability to comply with the discovery request. He doesn't have the ability to comply with the requests. Circumstances are not within his control with which to produce the documents.

And classically, Mr. Abbott, the attorney for the defendant says and I must quote, "If a party cannot produce, courts do not require a person to do the impossible. Therefore the motion to compel production should be denied."

Jack Neighbors and his father George were both brokers. Were they not required by the Real Estate Commission to keep a copy of their settlement statements?

I have to wonder in this year of 2003 how Elliot Spitzer, the New York Attorney General would have reacted if the lawyers for Arthur Anderson had told him that they had no records –therefore they couldn't produce. Not a good excuse.

LADIES AND GENTLEMEN OF THE JURY

Please let me prevail upon you to ponder these very serious concerns of ours.

- Who is concerned about the liability of the *limited partner?*

- The Neimay partnership started in 1975. This is 1986. The Executor says, under oath, there aren't many records! He can't produce what he can't find. Where are the records?

- How does the CPA for the partnership do an audit – even an "unaudited" audit, without records?

This is beginning to smell like the mother of all scandals – A COVER-UP. All of you in the public know that a COVER-UP is worse than the crime itself. If not, you didn't watch the national news about the WHITEWATER COVER-UP IN ARKANSAS that almost toppled a sitting President. It may have been more newsworthy than ours but there is not a dimes worth of difference. It's costly for the judicial system, which is mostly funded by the taxpayers. Extremely hard to put a price on it! So I'm thinking ---

Tom White, the Neimay partnership attorney is at the time reorganizing.

Jack Adams, the Neimay CPA, has sold his firm to Johnson and Burgess Company.

Planters National Bank and Peoples Bank, the two banks involved with this lawsuit, are talking about a merger.

And we are trying desperately to get discovery.

The New College Edition of the American Heritage Dictionary, which happens to be the one I have handy, gives the definition of MERGE as "to cause to be absorbed so as to lose identity. To blend together so as to lose identity."

Dear, dear God. Where are those settlement statements and where are the bank records that we can't get and what are they going to blend into? Are they going to lose their identity?

In October of 1985, we decided *ENOUGH IS ENOUGH*. We filed a petition to revoke the letters testamentary of John Neighbors in the George Neighbors estate.

- The 90-day inventory and all of the annual reports had been late – to the extreme.
- The fiduciary had failed to properly manage the estate assets.
- The fiduciary had failed to make prompt and accurate accountings to the *limited partner.*
- The fiduciary had failed to maintain accurate records regarding estate receipts and disbursements.
- The fiduciary had commingled estate assets and Neimay Partnership assets.

We called for a hearing with Betty Mann, the Clerk of Court who is responsible for overseeing and approving estate action. Clearly she should be concerned. She had a responsibility to the public who elected her to oversee these estates and be sure they were being handled properly.

CHAPTER 7

EFFORTS TO GET ESTATE RECORDS FROM THE

CLERK OF COURT

Chris Payne, the Planters Bank personal banker of Jack Neighbors wrote a letter to Betty Mann, the Clerk of Court, to be sure to let her know that Planters Bank was *very satisfied* with the handling of the estate *ACCOUNTS.*

LADIES AND GENTLEMEN OF THE JURY

WAIT A MINUTE! Did the personal banker say accounts – as in plural?

Remember this is the personal Planters banker who was the author of the infamous $40,000 "unsigned" personal note of George Neighbors. Remember the note was cleverly paid off behind the scenes by Tom White and the executor using Neimay partnership money, which was being retained in both of their trusts accounts.

The letter from Chris Payne explicitly informed the Clerk of Court that the executor had opened ***TWO*** estate accounts.

Planters National Bank

Post Office Box 661
Nags Head, North Carolina 27959

Telephone 919 441-5561

FILED

1986 NOV 13 AM 9: 11

DARE COUNTY, C.S.C.

BY _____

Planters Bank

November 5, 1986

Mrs. Betty Mann
Clerk of Court
Dare County Courthouse
Manteo, N.C. 27954

Subject: Estate of George W. Neighbors, John B. Neighbors, Executor

Dear Betty:

This letter is being written at the request of the above referenced executor to evidence our opinion of the manner in which he has handled the estate affairs relative to the bank.

On August 5, 1983, the executor opened the Estate of G.W. Neighbors, John B. Neighbors, Executor, account #316-156-0, and on August 7, 1984, he opened an account entitled "John B. Neighbors, Exec for the George W. Neighbors estate" (Kitty Dunes Heights) account #321-142-3. From the standpoint of the bank, both these accounts have been handled satisfactorily.

The debts that were owing Planters National Bank by George W. Neighbors at the time of his death were assumed by the executor on behalf of the estate and were paid in full in a satisfactory manner on the 2nd day of April, 1985. On December 23, 1985, the bank made a loan to the estate of George W. Neighbors for the purpose of completing the payoff on an Edenton house. This loan has been reduced in a systematic and satisfactory manner with a current balance in the low five (5) figures.

In summary, both the deposit and loan relationships established by the executor on behalf of the estate of George W. Neighbors have been handled in a satisfactory manner.

Sincerely,

S. Chris Payne
Vice President

SCP:epm

Stephen A. Midgett
Notary Public

(On May 15, 1986 under deposition Jack stated, "I have another account with a similar name in the same institution. I established a second account to keep the monies from Kitty Dunes Heights subdivision separate. There's a silent partner involved. I felt it would be a whole lot better to have a separate set of records for that partnership, a totally separate set of records." When asked by John Morrison "Who is that silent partner?" Jack Neighbors said, "Henry Atkins from Washington, DC.")

What the Clerk of Court should have picked up on *immediately* was that she was only monitoring *ONE* estate account and not doing a very good job of that. The other estate account was being hidden from everyone, *especially the government.* The only people who appeared to have knowledge of that hidden estate account were the Original 4, the executor and now the Clerk of Court. In fact, the Executor now had a *THIRD* account that he was using to commingle with the two estate accounts.

I truly believe the executor, with the training of the Original 4, is becoming a chip off the old block.

Believe me, this commingling became a nightmare for all of them – and of course, impossible to audit – even for a creative accountant. The interesting thing about the hidden account, that was being used to commingle with the "reported" estate account, was that it involved *just* Kitty Dune Heights properties – according to Chris Payne, Vice President, Planters National Bank.

Now, try to follow this carefully. *KITTY DUNES HEIGHTS* was a development next to Kitty Dunes Village (a Neimay venture). Kitty Dunes Heights was a partnership between George Neighbors, our **general partner** and Jack Adams, our creative Neimay CPA. It was called ADORS – Adams and Neighbors. *What a web they weave!* George and Adams had a falling out during this venture and George ended up with ADORS – of course. One of the last checks George stroked to Adams noted *GRAFT* on the stub. *Wonder what he meant by that?*

Now that George is dead, Jack Neighbors, his executor, *established* this second estate account just for Kitty Dunes Heights. *The banker said so.* The executor just forgot to report it to the Clerk of Court. Jack Adams is still everybody's accountant whether they are dead or alive. And he was the partner in the real estate venture that was not being reported to the estate. A lot of checks were written to Jack Adams and some cash checks for Tom White. It appears Tom White was the attorney for Kitty Dunes Heights. One thing you can always count on – these boys get paid – one way or another.

Many tricky creative transactions happened between the reported estate account and this Kitty Dunes Heights unknown and unreported account.

We were granted a hearing. We asked Betty Mann, the Clerk of Court, for the records to the estate because we have a legitimate lawsuit against the estate. We were being stonewalled from every angle and she just absolutely denied us our legal rights. When we walked out of her office, I looked at John Morrison, our attorney and said "John, doesn't that offend you? She just denied us our legal rights!" He didn't answer – because he didn't have one.

I was told at that time that Betty Mann had previously worked for Planters Bank.

On November 21, 1986 at 11:22 p.m., the Clerk of Court, in a formal filed order, not only denied us our rights but also ordered that we pay the cost of this action. *She said that Harold B. Mays is not an interested party and has no capacity to sue and no right to inspect the records of the estate, other than the public records.*

This was ENTERED on 13th of November 1986 and signed by Betty S. Mann, Clerk of Superior Court of Dare County.

LADIES AND GENTLEMEN OF THE JURY

What the Clerk of Court and Mr. Abbott did not realize was that that particular day was not a good one to try to intimidate us. That particular day, November 13, 1986 happened to be exactly six years to the day that our son has been missing off the Coast of Cape Hatteras – still to this day a mystery. It was not a good day to take away our rights.

I was getting real tired. My abnormal drive needed fuel. They just provided it.

I would get those estate records with or without them. And the Clerk of Court should not hold her breath for payment of those court costs.

Just five days after denial, we went back to court again to try to get the estate records.

We had filed a Motion for Removal of John Neighbors as Executor of the Estate but after a lot of thought about the mess they were making and the web they were weaving, we decided to give a notice of voluntary dismissal to that motion on February 3, 1987 in open court. *Let them live with it.* The defendant and his group were very pleased at this dismissal because they thought we had given up on getting the estate records. They thought the coast was clear. They read the signals wrong!

About this time, Jack Adams, our CPA, sold his business to and joined the accounting firm of Johnson, Burgess and *ADAMS*. The executor is feeling a little more confident and doing a few creative things on his own by not consulting with the Orig 4 and by gosh on February 12, 1987 he once again wrote a note to PLANTERS NATIONAL BANK giving the new accounting firm authority to have full access, copies of or any other data on checking accounts #3146278 and #3054756 held in the name of *Neimay Limited Partnership.*

2/12/87

To: Planters National Bank

This letter I am giving full authority

to the firm of Johnson, Burgess and Adams CI.

to have full access, copies of or any other

data on checking accounts # 3146278

and # 3054756

held in the name of Reimay Limited Partnership

Thank you for your cooperation.

Sincerely

John B. Neighbor
Executor for the Estate of
George N. Neighbor, General Partner
Reimay Limited Partnership (deceased)

What Jack evidently didn't know was these two accounts were *not* in the name of NEIMAY. Neimay funds were only commingled throughout. In fact, they were in the names of George and Jack Neighbors. It was beginning to surface that Jack was more confused about the Planters accounts than we were.

If Jack had no connection with Neimay, then why was he making any Neimay decisions? How can he legally give Johnson, Burgess and *Adams* permission to get all the information they wanted from the bank about Neimay accounts? We couldn't get anything from anybody and the **limited partner** was legally the only remaining partner.

LADIES AND GENTLEMEN OF THE JURY

I am sure you are aware by now that I *really* want those bank accounts!

CHAPTER 8

AUTHORITY GRANTED TO EXAMINE COMMINGLED

ACCOUNTS

On March 9, 1987, in response to a court order to produce *bank records*, Jack Neighbors hauled several boxes into John Morrison's Elizabeth City office. O. C. Abbott was standing militarily by the defendant's side and appeared to be there for the duration.

They evidently thought the duration was going to be short.

As I was flipping through the documents, I noticed that Jack had brought me *more* than I had requested. Suddenly I realized that he had brought me some of his father's commingled accounts that had extensive Neimay activity in them. He said he found this old box in a closet.

I tried not to show my excitement but I made up my mind *that very moment* that I would copy every single document.

I had the right to do that.

Jack Neighbors had no idea what he had brought me.

Neither did his attorney.

Neither did the Original 4.

I firmly believe Jack was following bad advice. And I believe all of the Big 4 had their own agenda.

About the third day, O. C. starting griping about being there so long. He started leaving Jack and me alone because he had other "emergency" work to do. Then Jack started leaving me alone because he too had other emergencies. This was my one and only emergency at that time. I was very, very concerned about copying all of the Planters Bank checks from all of the accounts. I was having real trouble putting Planters loan information together because the loans were so convoluted. I liked this discovery because the checks were originals. Before the electronic age banks always sent back your original checks with your statement. You could tell a lot more if they were originals. You could catch white outs and other tampering.

On Friday, O. C. Abbott told John Morrison that he was *going to take* the discovery. He personally decided we had been allowed enough time. I was *very upset* when John told me. I had been having a lot of trouble with his copier and I wasn't nearly finished. I blatantly asked him "Whose side are you on anyway John?" "Have they got you in their pocket?"

At that exact moment, high noon on Friday, John Morrison came up with a "brilliant" idea. He suggested that Judge Winberry, the judge who gave us the discovery, was in Pasquotank Court and he could go over there and ask for a temporary restraining order.

His brilliant timing didn't impress me but the temporary restraining order that Judge Winberry granted us did!!

I filed an affidavit and provided bond money so these crucial original Planters Bank checks could go under lock and key with Betty Mann, the Clerk of Court. Needless to say, O. C. Abbott was very, very upset with John Morrison's actions.

Chances are the Original 4 didn't like it either.

The past week had proven to be very stressful for me but very informative. O. C. had been rude and arrogant to me from the beginning of this lawsuit. I had known him for a long time. He was a late blooming attorney and he was a good ole' boy or a wannabee. I think he failed to realize that his arrogance could prove to be very costly later in life – maybe even as late as the year 2004.

I further confirmed, to myself, that Jack Neighbors was not really a bad guy but was definitely in a bad bind with some bad guys. My opinion is that they tried not to leave him alone with me for very long for fear he would innocently tell me some truth that might get them in trouble.

So on Friday at 5:00 p.m., the same day as the temporary restraining order, I looked at John Morrison with thorough disgust and said, "I am exhausted. I am going to see my doctor." My doctor knew I was working on the Neimay case. He took one look at me and said "stress." He gave me some muscle relaxers and sent me home to rest for the weekend.

I copied the discovery the following week until I was satisfied I had it all. We sent the handpicked Planters National Bank checks to the Dare County Clerk of Court.

On March 13, 1987, O. C. Abbott was again very busy sending off a lot of motions and answers to the Dare County Clerk. *He was trying so hard to keep up.* He was asking for everything to be dismissed and *please just give him back* those Planters Bank checks that were under lock and key.

At this time, they were desperate to keep me from getting the *Kitty Dunes Realty Escrow Account.* Kitty Dunes Realty was George Neighbor's real estate company and was the account that held a lot of Neimay money. I was very concerned about commingling. *There were a lot of suspicious checks in that box that Jack found in the closet.* George had been the broker who allegedly mishandled most of the Neimay property. All of a sudden, without us asking, the officers of Kitty Dunes Realty were sending us affidavits saying they have nothing to hide.

That certainly raised my interest!

(It's interesting to note that several of these officers left Kitty Dunes Realty right after the trial ended. That would include Jack Neighbors' wife, who divorced him after 17 years of marriage.)

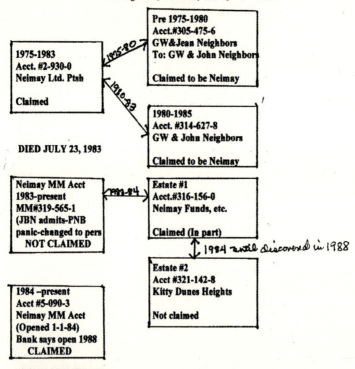

NORTH CAROLINA – DARE COUNTY
Harold B. Mays, Plaintiff
Vs
John B. Neighbors, Executor, Estate, & Personal

1975-1983
Acct. #2-930-0
Neimay Ltd. Ptsh

Claimed

DIED JULY 23, 1983

1975-80

Pre 1975-1980
Acct.#305-475-6
GW&Jean Neighbors
To: GW & John Neighbors

Claimed to be Neimay

1980-83

1980-1985
Acct. #314-627-8
GW & John Neighbors

Claimed to be Neimay

Neimay MM Acct
1983-present
MM#319-565-1
(JBN admits-PNB
panic-changed to pers
NOT CLAIMED

1983-84

Estate #1
Acct.#316-156-0
Neimay Funds, etc.

Claimed (In part)

1984 until Discovered in 1988

Estate #2
Acct #321-142-8
Kitty Dunes Heights

Not claimed

1984 –present
Acct #5-090-3
Neimay MM Acct
(Opened 1-1-84)
Bank says open 1988
CLAIMED

KEY PARTICIPANTS
George Neighbors
Norman Shearin - Attorney
Tom White-Attorney
Jack Adams-CPA
Ray White – Planters Bank
Chris Payne – Planters Bank
Jack Neighbors-Executor

I managed to start putting together the seven main bank accounts in which Neimay Partnership money had been *seriously* commingled. I was beginning to see the pattern.

I decided to call in the State Bureau of Investigation. I asked permission of John to meet with them in his office.

Very shortly after the request, a Special Agent from the Financial Crime Investigation Department of the North Carolina State Bureau of Investigation came to Elizabeth City and met with me in John Morrison's office. Melinda Coffin, the Special Agent, assured me in that meeting that she could get the estate records. She also informed me in that meeting that she had put lawyers and politicians in jail.

I must tell you LADIES AND GENTLEMEN OF THE JURY, that sounded GOOD to me.

I was studying the discovery day and night and hardly sleeping at all. I knew that what I had was a serious cover-up of real estate fraud involving lawyers, bankers, accountants and a realtor. I had a commingled account that dealt with an indicted drug dealer; many Planters Bank loans that were impossible to figure out because of the "vacuumed" deposit slips; Planters Bank loan money going in and out of all of the accounts automatically by the personal bankers and much more discovery waiting to be placed in the right slots.

I wondered if the bankers had WRITTEN permission from anyone in the partnership to automatically put loan money in and out of these accounts? Who was their oversight? Chances are the bank didn't have much paperwork either.

I just had this gut feeling that the Original 4 were expanding their camp. That is why I called in the SBI.

The confidence in Melinda Coffin was shattered in a few short months when H. P. Williams, Jr., the district attorney got involved and suggested to her that her file be *closed.*

General Court of Justice
Office of the District Attorney
First Prosecutorial District

H. P. WILLIAMS, JR.
DISTRICT ATTORNEY

TELEPHONE: (919) 335-0819

202 EAST COLONIAL AVENUE

ELIZABETH CITY, NORTH CAROLINA 27909

June 26, 1987

Special Agent M. C. Coffin
Financial Crime Investigations
North Carolina State Bureau of Investigation
Post Office Box 11308
Raleigh, NC 27604

Dear Melinda:

Thank you for your letter of June 8, 1987, regarding the
Neimay Ltd. Partnership. After having discussed this matter with
you it is my opinion that at this time there does not appear to be
any criminal violation by any individuals who are now living. For
this reason, I am requesting that your file be closed.

Sincerely,

H. P. Williams, Jr.
District Attorney

HPWjr:lkd

cc: Shirley Mays
    John Morrison

76

Can you believe that? He didn't even consult us.

He got the case dropped before she was able to get the estate records and maybe put some lawyers, bankers, accountants or an executor in jail. That really made me mad because I liked H. P. But I had to keep reminding myself that he was also a good ole' boy from Dare County. I felt sure he knew all of these players *real* well. The SBI agent had said in her letter to him that Shirley Mays suspected criminal activity on the part of John Neighbors, Thomas White, Jasper Adams and Chris Payne that was prohibiting the **limited partner** from taking over the partnership, which the partnership agreement, by law, permitted him to do.

Whatever the D. A.'s reasons were at that time, he appeared to me to be protecting the bad guys while clearly and blatantly taking away our legal rights.

I made myself a mental note while reading his letter.

WHATEVER GOES AROUND COMES AROUND.

The pressure was getting to John Morrison. He went to his doctor and got a statement TO WHOM IT MAY CONCERN that said he might not be able to prepare for a complex legal case by May 9, 1988. I *assumed* that was our trial. We should never make *assumptions*.

We were far from ready for our trial. John didn't appear to be pushing them hard at all.

We were now over three years into this lawsuit and everyone was still stonewalling. Most of 1988 was spent with us begging for records and them trying to get us into a trial with only pieces of discovery.

They all hate me by now and I'm not real fond of them either.

On August 4, 1988, O. C. Abbott wrote John Morrison to remind him of their pre-trial date of August 22. He suggested that they get together so they can meet their 22nd deadline. No one has followed a deadline for years but now, we're pushing deadlines. On August 4, O. C. Abbott, who was getting to be a real favorite of mine, answered our Motion to Produce insisting that it was a *further* harassment of the defendant.

Mr. Abbott should have gone to law school sooner. *He just doesn't get it.*

CHAPTER 9

COURT ORDERED ESTATE RECORDS

THE BREAKTHROUGH

This is probably the biggest breakthrough in the case so far. The Motion to produce the estate records went before Senior Superior Judge Herbert Small on August 22, 1988.

Instead of dismissing the motion as O. C. Abbott requested – because of our "further harassment"- Judge Small granted us the discovery. That meant we were going to *finally* get the estate records.

I couldn't believe my ears! By this time, I am sure a lot of people – including most of my family – thought I was getting obsessed with this case and might lose my mind over it. Judge Small knew me well and knew most of my family. I am sure he was aware that I would not be wasting my time in court if I didn't believe deeply in what I was doing.

He ordered Jack Neighbors to produce the estate records and have them in his office for my examination on or before 30 days. My attorney made arrangements for me to review the documents on September 9th. I walked into Kitty Dunes Realty on the 9th with my own copier and my own paper. I was never again going to be at the mercy of anyone's copier like I was in John Morrison's office when the darn thing nearly blew up.

First, I quickly examined what was furnished. *WAIT A MINUTE!* Things were too neat. I knew Jack was not in charge at that point. What "they" had done was try to disguise the second "unclaimed" estate account by switching the folders to confuse me. I started copying - folder covers and all - and didn't stop until the last piece of paper had been copied. I had learned, after all of these years, to not study the discovery while copying – *just copy every single piece of it and study later.*

Jack Neighbors wasn't there when I arrived. Evidently someone in his office called to inform him that I was there. He came flying up on his Harley – threw his helmet down – and made a total fool of himself. He might have scared his employees but I was way past the point of intimidation. *Besides, I liked Jack.* I never did understand why he did that. I had the court ordered right to be there! John Morrison had made the appointment, driven me to Kitty Hawk, dropped me off at Jack's office and left for another appointment somewhere. *I'm afraid they are getting to him!*

After studying the discovery, I immediately told John Morrison where the holes were and what we needed. Four and one half months later, he had done nothing. *I pushed to no avail.* I then hand- carried him a letter reminding him of the efforts of our accountant and me in preparing for this trial. I reminded him of the "holes" in the estate records and that we were at a standstill until we got them.

CHAPTER 10

ESTATE "ADJUSTMENT"

John Morrison was getting to be a real problem for me but I couldn't let him off the hook. We were too deep in this lawsuit and who would be dumb enough to step in at that point. No one in his or her right mind! John was having trouble in his own law firm so he struck out on his own and moved into an office at Peoples Bank. *Besides, he was on a retainer with them.* At this point, I was getting more concerned because Peoples and Planters were talking merger. I was still wondering about Morrison having a conflict. He again assured me he didn't and *if it got to that*, he would drop his small retainer with Peoples. I trusted that he would be good to his word.

The defendant and his people must have been getting worried because they engaged the services of a well-known expensive tax attorney whose firm had been affiliated with Peoples Bank in Rocky Mount. They needed an <u>adjustment</u> to the estate to include the <u>second unclaimed account</u> that I had discovered in Jack's office that day when he *wanted* to throw his helmet at me. *Chris Payne had said Planters was satisfied with the way these accounts had been handled. I wondered if Peoples Bank was just as satisfied. Maybe not.*

I was auditing my discovery fast and furiously at the same time that they were adjusting their estate information and you know what? They didn't get it all. Evidently, somebody was not leveling with the expert tax attorney they hired. My audit was much more accurate than theirs and I'm not even an accountant. *I'm just honest.*

The new adjustment that involved Kitty Dunes Heights covered the period from July 1, 1983 to June 30, 1987 and was dated 11-10-88– over four forgotten IRS years. The signature on the adjustment was Debbie J. Burgess, CPA – the firm Jack Adams sold to – *BUT* it was initialed by JA. Remember Kitty Dunes Heights was a development (ADORS) between

George Neighbors and Jack Adams. Adams appeared to be cleaning up his own mess. He certainly should be the most informed since he was a partner. This adjustment that was sent to the Clerk of Court was dated November 10, 1988. I'm not sure whether this was before or after Jack Adams lost his license. It doesn't really matter. Either way, the figures are wrong.

MESSAGE

TO:

L. Burgess
c/o Clerk of Court
Post Office Box 1000
Manteo, NC 27954

FROM:

JOHNSON, BURGESS & COMPANY
Certified Public Accountants
POST OFFICE BOX 1048
KITTY HAWK, NC 27949
Phone: (919) 261-2333

SUBJECT

Estate of George W. Neighbors
Kitty Dunes Heights

DATE   11/10/88.

Enclosed is a schedule of receipts and disbursements for

Kitty Dunes Heights for the period of July 1, 1983 to June 30, 1987.

The cumulative effect of prior partnership activity of $41,652.52

is calculated at the bottom of the page.

If you have any other questions, please call.

SIGNED   *Bobbie L. Burgess, CPA*

83

ESTATE OF
GEORGE WILLARD NEIGHBORS
File No. 83-E-104
Annual Accounting

	FYE 6/30/84	FYE 6/30/85	FYE 6/30/86	FYE 6/30/87	TOTAL
SCHEDULE OF RECEIPTS					
Sale of Kitty Dunes Heights lot less cost of sale	190.00	6641.00	2402.00	1935.00	3820.85
Interest on Notes Receivable	8320.95	10226.63	5871.63	1544.05	25963.26
TOTAL RECEIPTS	8510.95	16867.63	8273.63	3479.05	37131.26
SCHEDULE OF DISBURSEMENTS:					
Property tax – Dare County	1193.05	1099.75	1149.66	378.39	3820.85
– Kitty Hawk	342.38	396.91	120.18		859.47
– Nags Head	65.26				65.26
Intangibles tax	19.75	2.40			22.15
Professional fees – Joe Lamb, Jr. & Assoc.	550.00				550.00
– Robert A. Ladd, III				130.00	130.00
Survey		475.00			475.00
Accounting fees – Jack Adams		398.05	200.00	1200.00	598.05
Legal fees – Kellogg, White, Evans	10441.56			81.70	
– Johnson, Burgess, & Company		5433.51	56.00	584.87	13975.07
Interest – Jeff Banks	319.66				319.66
– Note Payable Chittum		9501.78			13101.78
– Note Payable Planters Bank	5600.00				47261.24
– Note Payable East Park	2879.04	9569.20	953.10	953.10	15683.36
– Note Payable Kitty Dunes Realty	885.20	14798.16		2741.06	12309.28
Closing costs on property sales					
Discounts on early note payoffs		41.44	1.50	7.10	
Bank charges	354.00	450.00			
Maintenance					50.04
Fence		5392.00			5392.00
Vepco – Underground service		450.00			450.00
Health Department			50.00		50.00
TOTAL DISBURSEMENTS	22649.90	47557.20	2530.44	6076.24	78813.78
GWN CAPITAL ACCOUNT (Beginning Balance)	62550.63	48411.68	17722.11	23465.30	62550.63
RECEIPTS	8510.95	16867.63	8273.63	3479.05	37131.26
DISBURSEMENTS	22649.90	47557.20	2530.44	6076.24	78813.78
GWN CAPITAL ACCOUNT (Ending Balance)	48411.68	17722.11	23465.30	20868.11	20868.11

Total Receipts 37131.26
Less Total Disbursements 78813.78
CUMULATIVE EFFECT OF -41682.52
PRIOR PARTNERSHIP ACTIVITY

About this second hidden estate account - I continue to call it hidden because evidently the state and federal governments did not know about it. Planters Bank and the Dare County Clerk of Court certainly knew about it. Remember the letter that Chris Payne wrote Betty Mann about being pleased with how the *two* estate accounts were being handled. Well, no one seemed concerned about it until I discovered – after great effort - the second estate account almost two years later. Now they are making an adjustment and simply sending it to the Clerk of Court without explanation – except to call if she has any questions. Somehow I don't think she'll bother them by calling and asking questions.

LADIES AND GENTLEMEN OF THE JURY

Why should anyone bother to follow the estate rules if everyone doesn't have to?

Does this mean that it is OK to steal – BUT – if you get caught, you must come clean or somewhat clean and make an adjustment? Is this what our judicial system has come to? What is the difference in that and a theft at the local seven-eleven?

If that is the case, why not give ALL criminals a chance to make an adjustment before sending them to jail.

Besides, the adjustment wasn't enough. I informed the clerk's office of that at the time of discovery.

The second estate account was opened, as Chris Payne and John Neighbors said, just for Kitty Dunes Heights. I checked with several of my friends who had handled family estates and they just didn't think a second estate account was kosher. *Especially* one that wasn't being reported.

What was so special about Kitty Dunes Heights that it had to be kept a secret? I think everyone was very happy about the way it was handled but me. I just don't know why these happy people worked so hard to keep this information from the government.

Anyway, everyone knows about it now!

CHAPTER 11

SETTLEMENT OFFER

We were still into delay, delay, and delay in getting discovery.

Lo and behold in March of 1989, Jack Neighbors, the executor, decides he is just tired of this whole mess and he is willing to settle for the big sum of $20,000. *But wait a minute*, there is still the issue of the small unbuildable lot in Kitty Dunes West – *THE PARKING LOT* – that needs to be quit claimed or something to somebody so the partnership can be dissolved and the estate can be closed and everybody can get back to business as usual - *WITHOUT SHIRLEY MAYS.*

Plaintiff's agent took about a New York minute to say no thanks to the generous offer. We had no idea what other liabilities might be involved. Bring on the long awaited accounting and banking discovery. It is our legal right to have that discovery. That is the *heartbeat* of this accounting lawsuit case! Let's take the facts to court.

CHAPTER 12

LEGAL EFFORTS TO GET BANK DISCOVERY

1990 was a busy and dangerous year for me. I was pushing hard to get the banking and accounting discovery. Boy – do these people play tough!

I told you about our Coast Guard Station. Did I tell you it was on the Historic Register? It is well posted as private property with *NO TRESPASSING*. I usually have no problems because it is such a visible property. One day in the late summer of 1989, my sister, my brother-in-law and I were standing on the side porch. A man drove into my drive – stuck his head out the driver's window – and shouted to me, "Are you going to be here this winter *ALL BY YOURSELF?*" I walked to the edge of the porch and told him to get off my property. I told him I was calling the Kitty Hawk police.

While I was in the house calling the police, he jerked his car out into the beach road and it died. It wouldn't start. I think the Lord shot his starter. He had to physically, by himself, push it back into my drive.

I had him arrested for threatening me. The Kitty Hawk police were there in a hurry. They told me that this man was a druggie, had picked a fight with a Nags Head policeman and had pulled a Highway Patrolman out of his car.

I was really wondering why he was picking on me!

On February 20, 1990, I took him to court – the same court in Manteo, NC where I had spent a lot of time since 1985 trying to get discovery. This person who threatened me tried to bribe the Kitty Hawk arresting officer right in the hall of the District Court – right before the trial. He told the policeman that he worked in a shell shop and he would let him take any of the shells he wanted if he would not testify. This is an Outer Banks story *but*

I swear that's the truth. The Kitty Hawk officer immediately told me and I said "Call Chief Morris – now." He did and his Chief said for him to go over to Superior Court and report the "shelling" bribe. He did.

Then the druggie's *attorney* approached me. He is a very good friend of mine from Elizabeth City. He is a long time family friend of my family and mine. He wanted to know if we could work something out. I said *ABSOLUTELY NOT.* This druggie threatened me in my own home and I didn't appreciate it.

I won in lower court so the druggie and *his attorney*, my friend, appealed, of course.

I went to Superior Court on the scheduled day of the appeal but some legal judicial magic happened. I sat there all day waiting. Finally the lawyer sitting next to me checked and for unknown reasons they had *rescheduled* my case for the end of the week. I called the DA's office to put them on notice that I wanted to be present in court when it came up. The DA's office promised to call me at least two hours ahead of the new schedule. I sat by my phone all week.

I went to our Station on Friday afternoon and read in the local paper that both charges on this druggie had been dropped. I thought to myself ----

WHAT GOES AROUND COMES AROUND.

I wrote the prosecuting Assistant DA a certified letter to complain. I requested a transcript of the proceedings. You guessed it. He never even acknowledged my certified letter. It appeared to me that the DA's office has one set of rules for the lawyers and total distaste for the public. *I was not their only victim.*

This is the same district attorney that suggested to the SBI that our Neimay case to get the estate records be *closed.*

Judge Thomas Watts, now deceased, was very adamant about getting this case to trial because of the age of it. He was determined to stop discovery but he was honest enough to recognize that we had a right to the bank discovery that we had been trying for years to get. On March 30, 1990, he ordered Planters National Bank to produce the records and for us to be finished with them by June 22, 1990.

The vice president and assistant legal counsel for Planters in their Rocky Mount office had designated a vice president in the Manteo branch as the proper party to be deposed to attest to the fact that original documents were being produced for discovery.

John Morrison wrote a letter, dated April 20, to Ray White, President of Planters in Manteo, informing him of his intention to depose that official. Ray White never answered anything – EVER. He never put anything in writing. If he did, I never saw it.

I believe some bankers think of themselves as being above the law. After all, bankers control the money and money is power.

Instead, John Morrison got a phone call from the legal counsel in Rocky Mount saying he *wasn't sure when* the Planters Bank official could be deposed. Appears someone had taken some emergency action behind the scene. John confirmed that phone call to me - in writing – at my request.

On May 18, John wrote a letter to the legal counsel expressing our concern that Planters National Bank *was not going to be able to meet the court's deadline to produce*. The legal counsel requested an extension until June 29, 1990. On May 21, 1990, he put this request in writing and said that the Planters official would be available for deposition.

They were buying a lot of time. I'm sure someone had checked the statutes.

On May 24, John went back to court to ask for an extension for the bank records. The judge gave him that and more – until July 13, 1990. I was very, very worried about the statutes running out.

On June 9, I again expressed my concerns to John about the bank and accounting discovery delays. I again asked John to acknowledge my letter – in writing.

I'm glad I had a strong feeling to document all these actions or inactions of John Morrison. Even though I like him as a person, his weaknesses were beginning to surface and they were definitely affecting our case. He never believed me when I told him about the conspiracy behind the scenes. He chose instead not to see what he didn't want to see. I think they call that tunnel vision. This weakness in him would start to become more and more visible.

It would be interesting for some knowledgeable legal reader to research this case and find out *exactly* when the statutes of limitation ran out for the bank boys. I feel sure it had something to do with their *not being able* to get the documents together.

Morrison informed me when the documents would be available at the Planters Bank Manteo branch. Something happened at this time that I didn't quite put together until much later. Morrison *DID NOT* depose anyone at Planters about these records. Don't know who might have strongly *suggested* that to him! I went there, by myself, with my own copier and plenty of paper. I did not receive a friendly welcome from the official who transferred Neimay money out of our account – after George's death – and transferred it into the Kitty Dunes Realty escrow account.

I don't think the official considered herself part of the problems of this lawsuit but the fact that she noted that the over $40,000 was not Neimay money was simply not true. She became a big part of the problem at that time. The check very clearly read Neimay Partnership. It was not a good transaction. I feel sure she was just following orders.

I set up my copier right by her office so she could see me the entire time. I didn't want to rock the bank.

SHE NEVER SUGGESTED TO ME THAT THESE COPIES WERE MINE OR THAT I COULD TAKE THEM HOME. I WAS NEVER TOLD

THAT I WAS BEING CHARGED FOR "those" LOUSY COPIES. I STOOD THERE FOR EIGHT HOURS COPYING THIRD OR FOURTH GENERATION MICROFICHE COPIES.

They were lousy – hardly readable – far from original – but no one had been deposed to say differently. I could tell, as I was copying, that the discovery appeared to have been vacuumed before it got to me. Without deposing anyone, we had no proof that they were not originals and we had no evidence of who had handled this discovery before I had access. Their efforts to intimidate John Morrison appeared to be totally successful.

CHAPTER 13

LEGAL EFFORTS TO GET ACCOUNTING DISCOVERY

In September of 1990, John Morrison, at my insistence, filed a Motion for Trial by Jury. I felt it might be our only hope because of the blatant corruption of our judicial system.

At the same time, we filed new motions for accounting discovery.

REMEMBER THIS IS AN ACCOUNTING LAWSUIT.

On October 2, 1990, O C. Abbott wrote John Morrison a letter stating his opinion of an incident involving me at the office of Debbie Burgess, CPA of Johnson and Burgess, the firm that bought the business of Jack Adams. O. C. was mistaken again and showed his lack of character by saying and I quote, "Debbie Burgess met with Doug Hollowell and Shirley Mays on Monday afternoon, September 26, 1990 at her office. As usual, Shirley Mays went right into her office, even though she was told that it was supposed to be a meeting between the accountants. Of course, this made no difference. To make a long story short, it appears that what Doug Hollowell wants, or better yet, what Shirley Mays wants, is the work product of Jack Adams. It will not be given to Doug Hollowell."

O. C.! It didn't happen that way at all. Debbie Burgess was extremely polite to us that day. I doubt that she told you any of that. Your intentions are very, very obvious. You guys have almost gotten to our attorney. Now you're trying to get to our accountant. I may not be the brightest bulb on the tree but you don't have to be a mental giant to know the elementary strategies of war. DELAY, DELAY, AND DELAY. THEN DIVIDE AND CONQUER.

I don't think anyone would question at this point that we have a legal war going on.

Mr. Abbott may have been getting his marching orders from others but his attempts to discredit me and his attempts to intimidate me were strictly of his own making. Someday I felt sure this would come back to haunt all of them.

On October 5, 1990, O. C. filed a Motion for an Order Ending Discovery. He's determined to stop me. He wants so badly to be their hero. He puts in his motion that I did not inspect the bank discovery at Planters until after July 13, 1990.

I would like to ask my readers a direct question.

IS THERE ONE SINGLE PERSON READING THIS BOOK WHO THINKS FOR A MOMENT THAT I WASN'T SITTING IN THE PARKING LOT OF PLANTERS NATIONAL BANK THE SECOND I WAS ALLOWED TO EXAMINE THEIR BITS AND PIECES OF DISCOVERY?

Again Judge Watts comes through on our discovery. He gives us the accounting we want but denies us a jury. It seemed strange to me that he would deny us that crucial right but he and O. C. Abbott discussed it for a few minutes, in front of John Morrison and me, during the court session and they decided we couldn't have a jury. *O. C. needed that win* because he was failing miserably in all of his other endeavors. Besides, at this point I would have felt sorry for a jury – having to listen to this confusion.

Again, as soon as possible my accountant and I were in Dare County knocking at the door of Debbie Burgess. This time, Doug Hollowell, out of the blue, also brought a copier. *He was catching on.* Thank goodness he did because mine broke down. It had been doing some serious copying. We went to Doug's car, got his copier and again every single "available" document was copied. Again, I could tell some serious vacuuming had taken place in the discovery. Or – the holes were there from the beginning.

The trial has been scheduled for February 18, 1991.

Can you believe it?

We had spent over seven years getting to this point and we were going to be moving forward without all of the requested discovery. I again wrote a letter to John Morrison documenting my concerns.

CHAPTER 14

TRIAL PREPARATION

It seemed almost unbelievable that we were finally going to trial. It had been over seven years since George Neighbors died. I had spent thousands and thousands of hours, day and night, in this pursuit of justice that turned into an absolute judicial nightmare.

Could this lawsuit have implications about my son that I didn't recognize ------------or was that just too big a nightmare to digest? I was sure, without a doubt that my daughters were beginning to think I was going to lose my mind. I would imagine my entire family was leaning that way. I have some very, very close friends who were always there for me. I know for a fact they were worried about me. Thank God, everyone hung in.

On the evening before the trial, our side checked in at the beautiful little bed and breakfast inn on the Manteo waterfront. This is the Land of Beginning – also the Land of the Pirates and *TOMORROW WAS THE BIG DAY*.

FEBRUARY 18, 1991

MAYS VS. NEIGHBORS

We had done our homework on Judge Russell Duke, the presiding judge. My attorney and I were pleased that we were going to have a fair Christian judge. He was also a Republican. That was a rarity in our judicial system because North Carolina is mostly run by Democrats.

My attorney and I had a lot of exposure in the area as Republicans. In fact, we were both appointees of Governor James Martin to the historical black university in our hometown of Elizabeth City – Elizabeth City State University. It was a real pleasure for me to represent the governor and my state in that appointed position.

CHAPTER 15

THE TRIAL AND RELATED EXHIBITS
February 18, 19 and 20, 1991

On the day of the trial, we walked about fifty steps across the street and entered the historic Dare County courtroom. People were milling about downstairs before court was called and my attorney and I got separated for a few minutes. He walked back to me and handed me a piece of paper. He suggested I read it right away. He said it was given to him by an attorney from the Kellogg, White, Evans, Gray and Lloyd firm. I casually took it from him, put it in my pocket and said I would look at it later. He appeared unusually nervous. I thought he just had the show time jitters.

It was time for court so we all casually wandered in as you do in a court setting. At the time that I was getting ready to sit down, a strange woman came up and got right in my face. She presented me with a piece of paper. I asked her name and she said she was Benita Lloyd with the Kellogg firm *REPRESENTING CENTURA BANK*. I looked at the piece of paper and it was a bill from Centura Bank (previously Planters) for over $1300 for copies that I had not received. I was trying to tell her, that when I went to Planters for my discovery, I took my very own copier and my own paper. That I stood in a corner where I could be watched continuously by a Planters official and that I didn't bother anyone. I owed them nothing for copies. *She didn't seem to care.* Her *unsigned letter* and Motion in the Cause to Tax Cost were freshly dated February 18 – the very morning of the trial.

KELLOGG, WHITE, EVANS, AND GRAY
ATTORNEYS AT LAW
KELLOGG BUILDING
P. O. BOX 189
MANTEO, N. C. 27954
TELEPHONE (919) 473-2171
FACSIMILE (919) 473-1214

February 18, 1991

REPLY TO:

Kill Devil Hills Office

MARTIN KELLOGG, JR.
THOMAS L. WHITE, JR.
CHARLES D. EVANS
E. CROUSE GRAY, JR.
RONALD E. DEVEAU
BENITA A. LLOYD
LEE L. LEROY

KILL DEVIL HILLS OFFICE
THE EXECUTIVE CENTER
3120 N. CROATAN HIGHWAY
SUITE 101
KILL DEVIL HILLS, N. C. 27948
TELEPHONE (919) 441-2336
FACSIMILE (919) 441-9414

DUCK OFFICE
SUITE C SCHOONER PLAZA
DUCK ROAD
KITTY HAWK, N.C. 27949
TELEPHONE (919) 261-7111
FACSIMILE (919) 261-0555

Mr. John S. Morrison
Attorney at Law
Post Office Box 436
Elizabeth City, North Carolina 27909

Re: Mays vs Neighbors et al
     Dare County File Number 85-CVS-173
     My file number 3400-004

Dear Mr. Morrison:

Our firm is general counsel to Centura Bank, successor by merger to Planters National Bank and Trust Company. Mr. John B. Fleming, Jr., who is a vice president and assistant legal counsel for Centura, contacted me on the afternoon of February 15, 1991, in regards to the above referenced matter. Mr. Fleming had learned that this case was scheduled for a non-jury trial at the regular civil session of Dare County Superior Court set for the week of February 18, 1991. Apparently, there is an issue concerning certain documents provided by Centura to your client, Mr. Harold Mays.

Mr. Fleming informed me that in response to an order entered by the Honorable Thomas Watts, Superior Court Judge, in this case, Centura has expended a number of hours researching its records and producing a large number of documents for your client. I understand that the cost of providing the documents was $971.60. In addition to this cost, there remains an outstanding cost of $333.69 for providing documents in connection with this same action several years ago. I understand that Mr. Fleming has contacted you at least twice recently on this matter to obtain payment. I am enclosing herein a copy of the original coping and research bill from Centura dated June 26, 1990; a copy of Mr. Fleming's letter to you of September 7, 1990, and a copy of Mr. Fleming's letter to you of January 28, 1991.

As stated in Mr. Fleming's letter of January 28, 1991, Centura provided the information in Judge Watts' Order as soon as the bank could and provided this information without the issuance of a subpoena. Mr. Fleming requested that your client pay the sums due by Friday, February 8, 1991. However, no payment has been forthcoming. I again renew Centura's demand that payment of the outstanding costs be paid prior to the hearing on the merits of this case.

If you have any questions, please feel free to contact me.

With best wishes, I am

Sincerely yours,

Benita A. Lloyd

BAL:rak
Enclosures
cc: Mr. John B. Fleming, Jr.

NORTH CAROLINA
DARE COUNTY

IN THE GENERAL COURT OF JUSTICE
DISTRICT COURT DIVISION
FILE NO. 85-CVS-173

*filed in open
Court 2-18-91
Anne Fee
Dep. CSC*

HAROLD B. MAYS,
PLAINTIFF

VS

THE ESTATE OF GEORGE W. NEIGHBORS,
JOHN B. NEIGHBORS, EXECUTOR OF THE
ESTATE OF GEORGE W. NEIGHBORS, AND
JOHN B. NEIGHBORS, INDIVIDUALLY,
DEFENDANT

MOTION IN THE CAUSE
TO TAX COST

NOW COMES Centura Bank, successor by merger to Planters National Bank and Trust Company, and moves the Court for an Order requiring the Plaintiff to reimburse it the sum of $1,305.29 for the production of certain discovery requests allowed under that certain Order dated March 30, 1990, entered in this cause by the Honorable Thomas Watts and in support of this Motion the undersigned shows unto the Court the following:

1. That on March 30, 1990, the Honorable Thomas Watts entered an Order which provided among other things that "after hearing the contentions of counsel, and examination of documents submitted by the various parties, the Court is of the opinion and does hereby so order that certain items of discovery should be allowed and others denied. The following discovery will be permitted by allowing Plaintiff's counsel at Plaintiff's expense to depose Planters Bank officers regarding the following Planters Bank records, pending further orders of this Court, to wit:" and the Order goes on to provide a list of various documents which the Plaintiff can discover. A copy of the Order entered by the Honorable Thomas Watts is attached hereto as Exhibit "A" and incorporated herein by reference.

2. That Plaintiff's counsel contacted Centura Bank to notify the Bank that the Plaintiff was being entitled to examine certain Bank records in the Bank's possession. A copy of a letter from Plaintiff's counsel is attached hereto as Exhibit "B".

3. That on April 30, 1990, Plaintiff's counsel again, contacted Centura Bank and expressed the urgency of the Bank producing the requested documentation as expeditiously as possible. A copy of the letter sent by Plaintiff's counsel is attached hereto as Exhibit "C" and incorporated herein by reference.

4. That Centura Bank complied with the Discovery Request and researched its records and produced copies of the requested documentation on or before June 26, 1990. That 83 hours of research time was expended in locating the documentation. That the total copy costs and research time

1

totalled $971.60. That a copy of the bill submitted for the charges is attached hereto as Exhibit "D" and incorporated herein by reference.

5. That since June 26, 1990, the Plaintiff has not paid Centura Bank for its costs and expenses incurred as a result of producing the Discovery information for the Plaintiff.

6. That the Plaintiff has not paid for the prior information produced several years ago which cost Centura Bank the sum of $333.69. A copy of the letter dated September 7, 1990, from Centura Bank to Plaintiff's counsel demanding payment of the sums is attached hereto and incorporated herein by reference as Exhibit "E".

7. That again, on January 28, 1991, Centura Bank, by and through John B. Fleming, Jr., Vice President and Legal Counsel for Centura Bank, made another demand on Plaintiff's counsel for payment of said expenses. A copy of Mr. Fleming's letter of January 28, 1991, is attached hereto as Exhibit "F" and incorporated herein by reference.

8. That the total sum of $1,305.29 remains outstanding and owing from the Plaintiff for Discovery produced by Centura Bank on the Plaintiff's behalf.

NOW, WHEREFORE, Centura Bank respectfully requests that the Court enter an Order providing that the Plaintiff pay these expenses to Centura Bank on or before a specified date and that the Court render such other and further relief as it deems just and proper.

This the 18th day of February, 1991.

KELLOGG, WHITE, EVANS & GRAY

By: _____
Benita A. Lloyd
Attorney for Centura Bank
3120 N. Croatan Hwy., Suite 101
Kill Devil Hills, NC 27948
Telephone: (919) 441-4338

2

CERTIFICATE OF SERVICE

This is to certify that I have this date served all other parties to this action or to their attorneys in their attorney's representative capacity with a copy of the foregoing in the manner prescribed by Rule 5 of the North Carolina Rules of Civil Procedure by:

Delivering (Handing a copy to the attorney or party or by leaving a copy at the attorney's office with a partner or employee).

Persons Served: John S. Morrison
                    Attorney at Law
                    606 East Main Street
                    Elizabeth City, North Carolina 27909

                    O. C. Abbott
                    Attorney at Law
                    P. O. Box 365
                    Elizabeth City, North Carolina 27907

This the 18th day of February, 1991.

Benita A. Lloyd

3

She said if I didn't pay her right then, this would go in the judge's court file and it would be the first thing he would see. I was extremely frustrated and looked around for John Morrison. I needed legal advice. *He was nowhere to be seen.* I now believe he was in the men's room throwing up. One of Kellogg's top attorneys, Tom White, our partnership attorney, was going to be testifying at this trial. Three of Centura's bankers (previously Planters) were going to be testifying. They had stonewalled us since 1983 and this was 1991. And the Kellogg firm and the bank were presenting me with this bill for lousy copies that I did not receive - in court - that morning - before the judge appeared? How blatant can they get?

This was definitely hardball on the part of the Kellogg law firm and the Centura Bank that they were representing and I didn't appreciate it.

I HAD BEEN FIGHTING THIS CORRUPT JUDICIAL SYSTEM FOR A LONG TIME ON MY HANDS AND KNEES.

I wrote a check, in protest, and prominently put that notation on my check.

I would like to mention at this time that after the trial was over, I complained to the Commissioner of Banks about the timing of this action. John B. Fleming, Jr., Vice President and Legal Counsel for Centura Bank, said, in an answer to their inquiry, "At the time we asked Benita Lloyd to file the Motion in the Cause referred to above, I was unaware of Tom White's previous involvement with Neimay Limited Partnership or with the Estate of George Neighbors, and our use of that firm was entirely unrelated to that previous relationship. Ms. Mays did agree to pay the cost shortly before court convened. Because the motion had been filed, it was, of course, in the court file when it was reviewed by the trial judge."

The legal counsel for Centura needed to do more homework before reporting to the Commissioner of Banks. There was NO stamped recording of the motion so there was no recorded time of action. There was a handwritten filed notation that it was filed in open court on February 18, 1991. Benita Lloyd was in such a hurry that morning that her letter was not even signed.

It was like a hit and run legal move by the Kellogg firm and Centura Bank. The unsigned letter and the motion were both dated February 18 – that morning. It was definitely a last minute desperation move by the lawyers and the bankers. *You can be sure it was the first thing the judge saw.*

It must have slipped the mind of this counsel for Centura, who, I believe, was the previous counsel for Planters National Bank, that on March 22 of 1985, John Morrison had written the president of Planters National Bank "that Mrs. Mays has been authorized to examine the books and records of the Neimay Limited Partnership for purposes of facilitating an accounting." A trip was then made shortly after that letter to Rocky Mount at which time, John Morrison and Shirley Mays met with the president of the bank, Ray White's manager *and the Planters National Bank's counsel.* It was quite a meeting! Ray White's manager was the lead talker in that meeting until I started explaining the infamous $40,000 personal note and how it was incorrectly paid with Neimay money. Abruptly, Planters' counsel called the manager into the hall and when they returned, *counsel took the floor.* I told them everything about the problems with Neimay, Tom White, Ray White, Chris Payne and Planters Bank in general. Their counsel was very nice and offered to do whatever he could to assist us. *I felt sure he would remember that meeting!*

I feel sure that was the same counsel who was now telling the Office of the Commissioner of Banks in 1991 that he was "unaware" of Tom White's previous involvement with Neimay Limited Partnership or with the Estate of George Neighbors. I had felt confident after that Rocky Mount trip that they were all aware of Neimay, Tom White, the Estate of George Neighbors and all of the problems involved with not being able to get bank records from Planters Bank. And about all of the commingling in those accounts? *How could he forget that meeting?*

Also, in that letter to Ms. Phyllis A. Stephens, Special Assistant to the Commissioner of Banks, State of North Carolina dated September 24, 1991, Mr. Fleming said, in response to my Exhibit 9: "At one time, Ray White, City Executive for Centura Bank, was involved in a real estate partnership by the name of Sea Ventures Company. Tom White, Norm Shearin and others were also partners in that partnership."

107

Back to the trial. When the confusion was over, John Morrison appeared just as quickly as he disappeared and sat beside me. Needless to say I was in a state of "what in the heck is going on?" I was beginning to doubt my attorney with my every thought. I just hoped he was physically going to make it through the trial.

The bailiff called out for us to stand and we all stood with respect. The next thing my attorney said to me was "Good God – it is George Fountain." I thought John Morrison was going to pass out. I asked him who was George Fountain? He was white as a ghost. He said I'll tell you later.

The court then took a short break before our trial started. My attorney began talking at breakneck speed telling me some of the tales that go around the legal circles about this legendary judge. He was called "Shoot From the Hip George Fountain." It was obvious John had been put in an unbearable position of intimidation. I told him how very upset I was with Centura and the Kellogg firm and that he knew I didn't get those copies. He informed me, for the very first time, that they had delivered those copies to his office a few days earlier and he had not had a chance to inform me. I knew *at that very moment* that the earlier morning courtroom action by Benita Lloyd of the Kellogg law firm and Centura was definitely planned to influence the judge's opinion of me and intimidate my attorney. They succeeded. I couldn't wait for *their turn to testify in court.*

The court came to order at 12:20 p.m. on February18, 1991 and the judge spoke first.

The following is taken directly from the trial transcript.

The Court:	Mr. Morrison?
Morrison:	Yes, sir.
The Court:	I've not looked at the file in your case.
Morrison:	Which case is this, your Honor?
The Court:	This is Mays against Neighbors.
Morrison:	Yes, sir.
The Court:	But I understand that it's largely an amount of accounting; is that right?
Morrison:	That's correct, Your Honor.

The Court:	Well, I never studied accounting as such. I think you need a referee in the case.
Morrison:	Well, Your Honor, considering there are two accountants, three accountants under subpoena here, we are prepared to proceed. Although I concede the discovery has been voluminous, we have tried to condense it down as far as possible. And I believe we could proceed with it. And my clients would strongly desire to do so. I have prepared a memorandum of law for Your Honor's research. I too was unfamiliar with accounting before getting into this case.
The Court:	Yeah, but you've had a year or so to get ready for it.
Morrison:	Several years, Your Honor, in candor. I state this to the Court, if you would like to read my memorandum, either party has the right to ask for reference.
The Court:	Right.
Morrison:	-under the Rules of Civil Procedure and under the common laws and equity laws of the county. However, no such motion has been made.
The Court:	Well –
Morrison:	The Court—
The Court:	It doesn't require a motion from either party.
Morrison:	I was getting ready to say the Rules of Civil Procedure give the Court the authority on its own to order an accounting. However, that is not mandatory.
The Court:	I understand.
Morrison:	It's in the Court's discretion. And this case has been pending a long time. We have got with us this evening people from out of state and so forth.
The Court:	Let me look at the file a minute so I can be more in tuned to what we ought to do about it.
Abbott:	May I say a couple of words?
The Court:	Yes, sir.
Abbott:	Your Honor, as I said briefly this morning, this is a complaint brought on account of a limited partner to the estate of a general partner and the heir of the general partner. In addition to what you see in the file, there are four or five depositions that have been taken.

Morrison:	That's correct.
Abbott:	And I guess it would probably be 15 or 20 witnesses at least involved, Your Honor. I don't know how many exhibits would be presented by Morrison or myself at this point. We do have the people here, Your Honor, and it would take us at least three days or so I guess. And you probably would have to take a lot of these documents with you home or someplace to render a decision in the case.
	We have not made a motion for reference, Your Honor, at this point because we never got the other side to agree to a referee. But, as I see it, you have three things you can do today. One of them is you can hear the case. One of them is you say, "I am not going to hear it" and continue it. And the other one is appoint a referee.
The Court:	Well, I am not going to continue it. There's no reason.
Abbott:	I am not asking for an continuance.
Morrison:	No, sir, we don't.
The Court:	I don't plan to do that.
Mr. Abbott:	We don't want a continuance. But those are the three choices that I think that you have. Your Honor, may I say this too. One of the reasons, I think, that an outside judge is here, that Judge Duke was originally brought here, was that Judge Watts and Judge Small did not want to try this case.
The Court:	Well, I understand that.
Abbott:	You are aware of that?
The Court:	Well, I am not aware. I just assume that because neither one of them would be here.
˙ Abbott:	Yes, sir. That's basically what it is. And, Your Honor, we are ready to go forward, if you want to referee.
The Court:	Let me read the pleadings and see where we stand on it.
Morrison:	Your Honor, may I respectfully make a suggestion, sir?
The Court:	Yes, sir.
Morrison:	You might find it more helpful to read the pretrial order which is in the file.
The Court:	I read the complaints; I will read the answer.
Abbott:	Your Honor, I have a copy if you would like to look at it.

The Court:	Well, I think I found it now. I found it.
Abbott:	All right.
	(Pause in proceedings while the Court reads.)
The Court:	All right. What about your pretrial order?
Morrison:	Well, I just thought that would simplify the issues.
The Court:	Well, where is that? Here it is. I've got it.
	(Pause in proceedings while the Court reads.)
The Court:	Are you asking for a jury trial in this case?
Morrison:	No, sir. We did not ask for a jury trial initially. Then as matters progressed at a later time we asked for one. And Judge Watts in his discretion denied trial by jury. Judge, in addition to all the exhibits listed on that pretrial, since that time there has been additional discovery and I received another box, I guess, Friday, last week any way, of additional possible exhibits in the case. Your Honor, although it indicates quite a bit on the pretrial, we have tried to distill our evidence to the minimum material.
The Court:	I see the last paragraph says you all have discussed the possibility of settlement. How seriously have you discussed it?
Morrison:	Seriously, Your Honor, but we are very far apart.
The Court:	Well, I tell you what we will do. I will start out with it. And I may ultimately appoint a referee for part or all of it. But I'll start out hearing it. And if we can complete it with me hearing it, I will be glad to do it. If I come to the conclusion that one party is indebted to the other, but it is going to take an accounting to determine the amount, I may refer it as to that. I just don't know. Let me get into it and we will see where we stand.
Abbott:	Your Honor?
The Court:	Yes, sir.
Mr. Abbott:	If your Honor has any notion that you may eventually have to get a referee, I would prefer, Your Honor, that a referee be appointed from the inception, because we will have to duplicate
The Court:	No, You don't know what I am talking about. If I conclude that there is an indebtedness, that the defendant owes the

	plaintiff something and I can't determine the amount, then I may appoint a referee to determine the amount. Okay?
Abbott:	Yes, sir.
The Court:	I didn't say I would.
Mr. Abbott:	No, sir. I understand you didn't say you would.
The Court:	It just depends on what I can do with it.
Mr. Abbott:	It's complicated. I am having a lot of – I've been with it five years now and it's very complicated even to me at this point. And I am going – if it would be appropriate for me to make a motion to put in a referee ––
The Court:	You can make the motion. I am willing to hear it. I don't want to get into something that's foreign to me which is accounting as such, but ----
Abbott:	That's what it's all about.
The Court:	But in the questioning of determinability, I don't mind doing that. And if it's clear that the amount is or if it's clear that there is no liability, I don't mind making that ruling.
Morrison:	All right, sir. You wish to proceed with this case first on the calendar?
The Court:	Well ----
Morrison:	I understand you have a jury trial.
The Court:	What is the practice here? Judy, you know what's the practice?
Ms. Stallings:	This week of court was set for this case.
The Court:	Okay
Ms. Stallings:	So really and truly this should go first.
The Court:	All right.
Morrison:	All right, sir. You want us back at 2:00 o'clock, Judge?
The Court:	Well, I didn't realize how late it was. I guess that's right off. (The Court recessed for lunch at 12:30 p.m.)

Analysis by author

- Right out of the gate, this judge says to our attorney, "I've not looked at the file in your case." And John says "which case?" *We only had one case!*

Before trial, I had been confronted by a Kellogg attorney who assured me that her motion will be the first thing the judge would see when he opens his file. The judge's first sentence was *"I've not looked at the file in your case."* Then John Morrison, who only has *one* case before this judge, says *"What case?"* I think he was concerned because he has a Public Censure in his North Carolina State Bar "file" and he doesn't know which "file" the judge is talking about. I think he was still in shock at that point and rightfully so. (I didn't find out about the Public Censure for another month or so when it was anonymously dropped at my door.)

- O. C. Abbott, the defense attorney, informed the judge that Judge Duke didn't show up and Judge Watts and Judge Small didn't want to hear this case. The judge replied, "I understand that." O. C. says, *"You are aware of that?"*

Of course the judge knew all about this case!

- Judge Fountain was very up front with the fact that he had never studied accounting, as such ------------------and we have an accounting lawsuit.

- John Morrison reminded the judge that he had a jury trial but the judge asked the court secretary what the practice was and she said, "This week of court was set for this case."

I would be surprised if this scheduled judge had not previously been informed that "this week of court" was set for this long, dragged out accounting case.

- Judges Duke, Watts and Small ride the circuit but I think Judge Fountain was partially retired. And Judge Fountain doesn't have any time to prepare for this trial? Not enough time even to read the answer to the complaint or the pretrial order before appearing. Several judges had been very involved with discovery for this case for six years. They did not want to hear it. *I think we're in trouble.*

We came back from recess at 2:00 p.m. The judge looked at the pleadings more carefully and remarked to Mr. Abbott "John Neighbors was never a partner in this?" Mr. Abbott replied "No, sir, Your Honor. He's the executor of the estate." Then the judge stated, "Right. Well, he's not a party except as executor." Mr. Abbot replied, "He's also listed individually."

The judge in the very beginning knew that John Neighbors was not a partner in Neimay.

THE FOLLOWING PEOPLE ARE LISTED IN THE ORDER IN WHICH THEY TESTIFIED IN COURT.

This was the first day of the trial - February 18, 1991.

Harold Mays, the Limited Partner, was first witness on the stand February 18,1991.

O. C. had no mercy. He was a family friend and he was well aware of our situation. He knew losing our son had blown our family apart. We were all trying to cope. Bud was having a real hard time. At the time of the trial, I believe he was in deep depression. He had just driven in from Indiana. This depression was evident to me because his answers were confusing. Of course, he had not been involved with the discovery of this case since he left the State in 1985 and this was 1991. He had a hard time reaching for the details of 1975. O. C. knew that and took advantage of it. *O. C.'s real target was me.*

Jack Neighbors was second and last witness on February 18, 1991.

Jack Neighbors didn't know much more than Bud because George had also kept him in the dark. He had a tough job as executor of the estate. He contradicted himself several times as to whether he had anything to do with Neimay before his father's death. During his *deposition on May 15, 1986,* Jack had told John Morrison that his father had wanted him to take over the businesses after his death.

Morrison:	In fact you became managing partner after your father's death?
Neighbors	Yes, sir, that was my understanding or that was his wish.
Morrison:	Whose wish?
Neighbors	George's
Morrison:	Did he ever tell you that?
Neighbors:	Yes.
Morrison:	When did he tell you that?
Neighors:	No specific time. It was mentioned in conversations that we had probably no sooner than three years before his death.
Morrison:	Approximately 3 years before his death your father told you he wanted you to take over and manage the partnership after his death?
Neighbors:	Indirectly, yes, sir, he told us to the point of maintaining family interest?
Morrison:	What do you mean?
Neighbors:	This could get way off the subject of Neimay. He felt that it was important passing from a parent to a child, he just felt that way, that part of the trade passing from father to child to grandchild is the way it should be. He felt that it should simply be the case and at that point he cut off and went in another direction.
Morrison:	That was just his personal feelings.
Neighbors:	His personal philosophy.
Morrison:	His personal philosophy?
Neighbors:	Yes, sir.
Morrison:	So he was discussing this with you before his death. He was discussing the various aspects of the Neimay business.
Neighbors:	No, that he just wanted me to take over the business.
Morrison:	Did you have a conference with Mr. Tom White, an attorney in Dare County, after your father's death about Neimay?
Neighbors:	Specifically, Neimay, I'm sure we have, yes, sir. I know we have.
Morrison:	After this conference with Mr. White was it your opinion that you should run the Neimay business or that it should be wound up or just what?

Neighbors:	My feelings were that I should wind it up as fast as possible and obviously operate or manage it in the meantime.
Morrison:	Did you become familiar with the partnership agreement?
Neighbors:	Not nearly as familiar as I should have gotten; of course things were different then.
Morrison:	You are aware that under the partnership agreement discussed, it was understood that the surviving partner should take over the partnership business?
Neighbors:	I am very aware of it now.
Morrison:	Could you explain to me why you wanted to run the business instead of following the partnership instructions?
Neighbors:	I didn't read it.

These are statements of Jack Neighbors under oath. There is no doubt that he was not familiar with the partnership agreement and felt that the business was to be his. He had consulted with Tom White, the partnership attorney and still was not informed. Jack gave many other damaging statements during the deposition and during the trial but one of the outstanding remarks of his had to do with the *limited partner* not being able to get Neimay records or settlement statements from him or Tom White.

Morrison:	Do you know of any reason why the records would be missing?
Neighbors:	Because they were never created in the first place.
Morrison:	If these records were never created then they were not transmitted to Mr. Adams for use in accounting?
Neighbors:	Whatever documents there were, were transmitted to Adams, I don't know how they were transmitted the information as to where the closing money went.
Morrison:	You understand that is my question, if you don't have the record, how can Adams make an accounting, if some of the records are missing?
Neighbors:	I know exactly what you're saying.
Morrison:	You don't have an answer to that at this point?
Neighbors:	Right.

Morrison:	What would be the reason for handling the transaction that way as you have just described rather than for a more formal presentation?
Neighbors:	Avoidance of attorney's fees.
Morrison:	That's a terrible thing you're saying, you know what?
Neighbors:	A capital sin, I believe, punishable by having to do this.

Analysis by author

Jack is very clear in his feelings both in his deposition and in the trial transcript. He did not have a close relationship with his father. But he still thought his father wanted him to continue the family businesses. When he said, "at that point, he cut off and went in another direction," I think he was referring to George divorcing his mother and marrying again. George's new wife was active in the business.

Jack didn't appear to have a high regard for the lawyers. At this time, there was a lot happening behind the scenes at Kitty Dunes Realty that the *limited partner* was not aware of.

The second day of the Neimay trial was February 19, 1986. Up for testimony were two lawyers, three bankers and three accountants.

Norman Shearin, the original Neimay Partnership attorney was up first the second day.

The following is taken directly from the trial transcript of February 19, 1991.

Morrison:	And you have been practicing in Dare County for how long?
Shearin:	Since 1972.
Morrison:	And your practice consists primarily of commercial and real estate orientation?
Shearin:	Business, right, commercial real estate.

Mr. Shearin had been subpoenaed for deposition in 1986 like Jack Neighbors, Jack Adams, Tom White and Chris Payne. Mr. Shearin didn't show up. I was not given a reason from John Morrison. He was only on the stand, under oath, for a few short minutes at the time of trial. One of the questions that Mr. Abbott put into the record was about the settlement statements of some of the oceanfront lots that Norman Shearin would have handled at the same time that he was a trustee on the Peoples Bank Neimay mortgage. Mr. Shearin's answer was that they followed a practice in their office of destroying files after ten years. He said that at the time Morrison contacted him for those settlement statements, even if they had previously existed, they would have been destroyed.

Norman Shearin wore two large hats with Neimay. He was the original partnership attorney and at the same time, he was one of the trustees on the $400,000 Neimay mortgage at Peoples Bank. The trustees had to supply release deeds. After handling the oceanfront lots, his only role, *I think*, was being the trustee at Peoples for the remainder of the mortgage. Further trial testimony --

Morrison:	And then it was financed with Peoples Bank. And I believe you were Trustee.
Shearin:	I think I was one of the trustees. I think maybe Frank Meadows, a lawyer in Rocky Mount was.
Morrison:	And in order for property to be sold by Neimay, you had to give release deeds of Peoples Bank?
Shearin:	Well, yes. You know, the bank actually approved and executed the release deeds and presented them to the trustees for execution.
Morrison:	And most of the land was originally sold on installment land sales contracts.
Shearin:	You know, I -----
Morrison:	All right, sir.
Shearin.	I simply am not certain. You mean contracts for warranty deeds, installment as opposed to a deed note, deed of trust?
Morrison:	Right.
Shearin:	Mr. Morrison, I don't have any specific recollection. But I do recall that a lot of the things that George Neighbors did and was involved in were sold on land contracts.

Morrison:	Now, you closed several of these transactions yourself where deeds were conveyed to people; is that correct?
Shearin:	I am sure we must have closed some of those transactions.
Morrison:	And was it your custom to send copies of closing statements to Mr. Neighbors' office?
Shearin:	Neighbors would have been the real estate firm. His real estate firm would have had a commission involved.
Morrison:	Yes.
Shearin:	Yes. It is our firm's practice, where a real estate firm is involved and is paid a commission, to supply them with copies of the closing statement, yes.
Morrison:	All right. Thank you I have no other questions.

Analysis by author

Jack Neighbors never furnished us any of the settlement statements from Norman Shearin because he couldn't find any and was not furnished any.

Meadow Austin, Planters Bank Operations Officer was second up second day.

The following is taken directly from the trial transcript of February 19, 1991.

Morrison:	How are you presently employed?
Austin:	Centura Bank.
Morrison:	And that was formerly –
Austin:	Planters National.
Morrison:	---- Planters National. That later merged with Peoples. That occurred just a few months ago.
Austin:	Mm-humm.
Morrison:	All right. 'And what is your current position with Centura Bank, ma'am?
Austin:	I am in charge of operations.

Ms. Austin is the Planters Bank official that was designated by the counsel at their main office in Rocky Mount to certify that all those copies I

SHIRLEY MAYS

copied were originals and who might have handled them before I saw them. She was never put under oath by John Morrison regarding that matter.

Ms. Austin was also the operations officer who handled a Neimay check for $40,233.75 on September 13, 1983. The transmittal slip said it was put in the Neimay account **in error** in JULY, was transferred out automatically in October and redeposited into the Kitty Dunes Realty Escrow Account.

O. C. Abbott, their attorney, then attempted to record "sloppy bookkeeping" in the records. Further trial testimony -------

Abbott: Ms. Austin, as I understand, what you are saying is that banks do make mistakes. And it could have been a deposit slip made to the account of Kitty Dunes and it got misplaced into the Neimay account?

Austin: That's a possibility.

Abbott: Did Mr. George Neighbors or did Kitty Dunes Realty have an account at your bank at the same time? Do you know?

Austin: Yes, they did. I don't remember the exact name of it, but I think it was Kitty Dunes Realty.

Abbott: Is it a normal practice when people have more than one account to bring several deposit slips together and deposit it at the same time in the same bank, different accounts?

Austin: Oh, yes. A lot of businesses do that.

Abbott: Okay. And you are satisfied that your note that you made back in 1983 is correct, that it was deposited in error to Neimay account. It should have been to the Kitty Dunes.

Austin: Yes, I am.

Abbott: Thank you.

Morrison: If I may on that?

Morrison: I believe you said you had no recollection of why this was done, though.

Austin: No, I don't. But I don't think I would have just up and done it without checking it out and ---

Morrison:	You think somebody would have asked if you called Mr. Neighbors and told him you did it?
Mr. Abbott:	Objection.
The Court:	Overruled.
Austin:	I don't remember, but I do have to make corrections in my job in accounts. And I think I would be careful and try to see that I was ----
Morrison:	I am certainly not accusing you, ma'am. I don't want to give you that impression. I am just trying to understand if you know of any reason why this was done that you recall specifically.
Austin:	No. I can't remember. The only reason that I say it was done is because we posted a deposit to the wrong account is what it appears.
Morrison:	All right. Thank you.

Analysis by author

It is my opinion that Ms. Austin was not aware of the "alleged" conspiracy going on in this lawsuit. I feel sure that she *would not* have intentionally become a party to it. I believe she was just following instructions that day from someone she trusted. She simply made a mistake. *That was Neimay money.*

It went into the proper account to start with. Then it went to Kitty Dunes Realty Escrow Account. Then it went to Tom White's Trust Account. It was then mishandled by Jack Neighbors and Tom White, in an improper closing with Billy Beasley, a local fisherman. The exact amount was applied to the closing, without the *limited partner's* knowledge.

The *limited partner* at this same time was trying to get the Neimay records. He knew nothing about this closing and definitely did not sign the deed.

Jasper L. Adams, the Neimay CPA is third up second day

The following is taken from the trial transcript of February 19, 1991.

Morrison:	And you are a certified public accountant; is that correct?
Adams:	Yes, sir, I am.
Morrison:	Are you still engaged in that practice?
Adams:	No, sir, I am not. I sold my accounting practice in 1975. Excuse me, 1986.

Morrison	You were the accountant to Neimay Limited Partnership from its inception in 1975 until what date, if that's correct.
Adams:	Yes, sir. 1975 through February of '86, when I sold my practice.
Morrison:	Now have you handled any Neimay affairs since then?
Adams:	Not that I can remember, no, sir.

Cross-examination by O. C. Abbott.

Abbott:	Yes, sir. Mr. Adams, you say you practiced accounting in Dare County for a number of years; is that correct?
Adams:	Yes, sir, I did.
Abbott:	And a good bulk of your practice is concerned with real estate subdivision work; it that correct?
Adams:	The majority of my practice, yes, sir.
Abbott:	And how many subdivision projects did you handle? How big was it?
Adams:	I handled the work for Kitty Hawk Land Company, who was the developer of Southern Shores. I helped set up and handle the work, until I sold my practice, for Martin's Point. I handled the work for First Flight Village for Nags Head Acres, for Old Nags Head Cove, for Kitty Dunes, for Kitty Hawk Landing, for the Landing, for Burnside Forest, for the original owners of Pirate's Cove, for Barrier Island Station, for the Wind Jammer Resort, for the Norman

Strand Resort, for High Dunes Resort, for the Seven Seas
Condos, Eagle's Nest Resort, Camp Shores Resort. I made
this list from memory. I didn't go back and look at my file,
so it doesn't include all of them.

Abbott:	Now you say you are familiar with the contract of Neimay Limited Partnership; is that correct?
Adams:	Yes, sir.

Abbott:	Your Honor, maybe we can go onto something else.
The Court:	Sure.
Abbott:	All right, sir.
Abbott:	Now, you were in a partnership with him at one time, were you not?
The Court:	With whom?
Abbott:	You were in a partnership with Mr. Neighbors, were you not?
Adams:	Yes, sir, I was.
Abbott:	And that was ADORS?
Adams:	ADORS Limited Partnership.
Abbott:	And once upon a time you did owe the partnership – not partnership, but Mr. Neighbors, about $36,000 or somewhere around?
Adams:	Yes, sir. In September of 1978 I purchased the Kitty Dunes Professional Center, which was an office building, from Mr. Neighbors and gave him as part of the purchase price my personal note for $45,000.
Abbott:	That was not part of the Neimay property.
Adams:	No, sir. And in July of 1984 I sold the property and the note to Mr. Neighbors. The estate was paid off.
Abbott:	That's what Mr. Morrison was referring to, I assume, a while ago.
Adams:	Well, the best I remember Mr. Morrison asked me if I owed money at the time I prepared the accounting. I didn't prepare the accounting until 1985.

*Regarding ADORS or Kitty Dunes Heights, I want to refer to a **deposition** dated June 10, 1986 –*

Morrison:	Now, do you know of any other estate accounts, do you know of two estate accounts being maintained, one for Kitty Dunes Heights and then a separate account for the Estate of George Neighbors?
Adams:	When Mr. Neighbors died there were 3 or 4 different accounts.
Morrison:	Tell us to your best recollection what those accounts are for?
Adams:	Without my files, I could not tell you. Again, I don't have that file with me.
Morrison:	Would you be able to give us that information at a later time?
Adams:	Yes, sir.

Adams did not answer the question about two estate accounts and to my knowledge, he never gave the information to John Morrison at a later time. This was in 1986. I discovered the hidden account in 1988.

Back to the transcript from the trial--

The Court:	I am talking about the amount that Mr. ----well, when you say Mr. Neighbors owed that, of course he had died in 1983. So that's been carried forward since 1983?
Adams:	No, sir. That's not right. Because ---
The Court:	What is right?
Adams:	From the date of Mr. Neighbors' death, if you will look on page 3 of 3, it shows the 40,000 that Mr. Neighbors put into the partnership prior to his death.
The Court:	Wait just a minute. Three of three.
Adams:	Yes, sir. It shows a $500 check. Mr. Neighbors passed away in July of '83. After that time, there is an entry for $3,573.30 which was a payment to Planters Bank on that $40,000 note which came from the Olds closing. Underneath that, there was a, on October 17, there was

	$19,908.25 that was paid to Planters Bank from the Beasley closing.
Abbott:	Mr. Adams, I believe you lost me.
The Court:	Wait just a minute. These are payments that were made after he died?
Adams:	Yes, sir, it was.
The Court:	Well, who was making these payments?
Adams:	Okay. In those three instances right there, Beasley was a sale of a piece of land the partnership owned. And the attorney paid the proceeds back in repayment of this $40,000 loan.
The Court:	Okay.
Abbott:	What are you referring to, Mr. Adams?
The Court:	Are you talking about the Olds closing, Beasley closing and Ryder closing?
Morrison:	What page are you on?
The Court:	It's on page 3 of 3. I was just wanting to know how they got paid. This young man here didn't actually pay them himself.
Adams:	Those three were paid ---
The Court:	From the lawyer's closing. Rather than paying the seller, they paid the bank.
Adams:	That's right.
The Court:	Okay. Go ahead.
Abbott:	Now, Mr. Adams, Judge Fountain asked you about what was paid after his death.
Adams:	Yes, sir.
Abbott:	Is that all that was paid after his death or was there some other things paid?
Adams:	Well, they are listed there on that page 3 of 3. And we've only talked about two of them. There are some more listed underneath that. On December 31st of '83, there was – excuse me—on March the 2nd 1984 that was a payment to Planters from the Anderson closing. There was March 30th, '84, that was a payment. It was check No 004 to Planters for George Neighbors. That was a check. That wasn't

deducted from a closing, okay. And then on February 29, '84

The Court: Well, how can that be a check ---oh, for George.

Adams: Check from the partnership to Planters Bank.

The Court: Well, who would have given that check?

Adams: Mr. Neighbors. Mr. Jack Neighbors had the checkbook.

Abbott: Now, Mr. Adams, were you here when Mrs. Meadow –

The Court: Austin

Abbott: I mean Austin.

Abbott: ---- was testifying?

Adams: I came in during her testimony, yes sir.

Abbott: Can you shed any light on the deposit slip that was made to Neimay and then put into the Kitty Dunes partnership or Kitty Dunes bank account?

Adams: In going through the records for the bank statements for 1983, there was a ---there was a deposit shown on the bank statement in September of $40,233.75. And then---

The Court: Into whose account?

Adams: Into the Neimay Limited partnership account. And then on October 7, 1983, there was what was shown as a check coming out of that account for $40,233.75.

Abbott: Did you trace that out to find out what that was all about?

Adams: In the bank statement there was a form that is an advice of debit showing where the money came out. I also --- during that period of time there was a sale of property to Billy Conrad Beasley.

Abbott: Do you have a statement?

Adams: Yes, sir, I do. And it shows on that settlement statement that there was received into escrow by check from Kitty Dunes Realty $40,233.75, which was the same amount of the deposit to Neimay in the draft of Neimay's account.

Abbott: Does that settlement statement show this $40,233.75 went – who would it go to?

126

Adams:	$8.00 was for Registrar of Deeds, release deed. $42.50 Registrar of Deeds, revenue stamps. $200 to Kellogg, White, Evans, Sharp Michael for preparation of deed release deed paying funds for a release. Peoples Bank and Trust Company release price $15,075. Planters National Bank $19,908.25, which was one of the payments on the 40,000 note we talked about earlier. And 5,000 retained by Kellogg, White, et als trust account for inheritance taxes arising from George W. Neighbors, $5,000.
Abbott:	Thank you, Mr. Adams.

REDIRECT EXAMINATION BY MR. MORRISON

Morrison:	Mr. Adams?
Adams:	Yes, sir.
Morrison:	You each year that you served as accountant for Neimay partnership, you would make postings and books of original entries; is that right?
Adams:	Yes, sir.
Morrison:	On an annual basis?
Adams:	Yes, sir.
Morrison:	Okay. And they would have supporting schedules with them?
Adams:	Yes, sir, they would.
Morrison:	Yet when an accounting was asked for, you went back, instead of giving all those annual accounts you had made at that time, you relisted everything?
Adams:	Yes, sir, I did.
Morrison:	Without supporting entries and ledgers, documents?
Adams:	Yes, sir. I did have the supporting --- my annual papers.
Morrison:	But you didn't forward those to us, did you?
Adams:	No, sir, based on what Mr. Abbott told me to do.
ABBOTT:	Objection.
The Court:	Overruled.
Abbott:	He wasn't supposed to do that.

Morrison: Why would you do that? Why wouldn't the supporting ledgers and entries and other documentation be supplied on a year-by-year basis rather than having to reduce the whole thing and copy it over manually?

Adams: I prepared an accounting based on the instructions from Mr. Abbott.

Morrison: All right, sir. Surely Mr. Abbott didn't tell you not to give us any supporting entries?

Adams: No, sir.

Morrison: Or documentation?

Adams: No.

Morrison: You made that decision.

Adams: No, sir, I did not.

Morrison: You didn't make a decision not to give us the supporting documentation?

Adams: No, sir, I did not.

Morrison: Why didn't we get the supporting documentation?

Adams: Because I didn't have the documentation at the time. I sold my practice and --- I am sorry.

Morrison: Excuse me. I'm sorry. I don't mean to interrupt you. You have the right to explain your answer. I apologize. Go ahead.

Adams: The only records I had were my work paper files. And I couldn't give those to somebody else because then I wouldn't have anything to support the work that I did.

Morrison: So at the time you made this accounting, you are telling us you didn't have the supporting documentation?

Adams: I did – in 1985 when I prepared the accounting, I had my work papers files from which I prepared the accounting from.

Morrison: But you didn't have the supporting documentation?

Adams: I didn't have the bank statements or contracts and all. There were at the office, Kitty Dunes Realty office.

Morrison: And you could have certainly gone back and gotten those?

Adams: The bank statements, sir?

Morrison: Yes.

Adams: Sure, They were in the office there.

Morrison:	So you made up this accounting from your notations?
Adams:	From my work paper files, yes, sir.
Morrison:	From earlier years.
Adams:	Yes,sir.
Morrison:	Rather than going back to the original documents.
Adams:	Yes, sir. It would have been --- I would have repeated work to have gone back to the original documents when I already had all that information in my work paper files.
Morrison:	Did you leave your work papers with Ms. Burgess?
Adams:	In 1986 when I sold my accounting practice, yes, sir, I did.
Morrison:	And did you copy those over?
Adams:	No, sir, I did not.

Analysis by author

I would guess, for sure, that our accountant from Pittsburgh, Mr. Rosenfeld, did not have access to "all of the books" when he visited the Outer Banks on our behalf. They just gave him what they wanted him to see. In my opinion, Jack Adams was well aware of what George was doing. In my opinion, Jack Adams *had to be* a party to the wrongdoing. In my opinion, the cover-up by an accountant is as bad or worse than the crime itself.

After the second ADORS estate account was discovered by the plaintiff's agent, an adjustment was made to the estate for the years 1983, 84, 85, 86 and 87. It was dated November 10, 1988 and was under the heading of Johnson and Burgess. It was signed by Debbie J. Burgess – but initialed by JA. Plaintiff's agent informed the Clerk of Court immediately because we had a lawsuit against the estate.

Jack Adams, under oath, said that the Peoples Bank note in Rocky Mount was paid off in June of 1983. And then he testified, under oath, that additional release payments – after payoff – and after George Neighbors death – had been taken out of closing statements from Olds, Beasley, and Ryder by Tom White, the Neimay partnership attorney. He showed them on his accounting to the *limited partner* s as *loans to George*, the deceased *general partner* instead of release payments to Peoples Bank.

129

Thomas L. White, Jr., Neimay partnership attorney is fourth up second day.

The following statements, under oath, are from the deposition of Thomas L. White, Jr. on September 12, 1986 at 10:00 a.m. in the Kitty Dunes Realty office of Jack Neighbors.

Morrison: Do you recall at the time of these conversations that we just mentioned what your advice was to Mr. Jack Neighbors and to Mr. and Mrs. Mays regarding who should wind up the partnership?

White: Yes.

Morrison: What was that advice, please?

White: Apparently there was concern about who would, in effect, step into the shoes of the general partner. And after looking through the partnership, it was my opinion that the partnership provided that the limited partner would have the right to purchase all the general partner's assets. But in my opinion they didn't provide the limited partner could step into the shoes of the general partner.

And; in fact, Virginia law would have the personal representative of the deceased partner would be the one that would step into the shoes of the general partner for the purposes of winding up the affairs of the partnership. And the partnership itself did provide, as does North Carolina law, that unless there is a provision otherwise that the partnership would be dissolved upon the death of the general partner.

Morrison: At that time the partnership should have dissolved?

White: That's right, and dissolution usually means winding up the affairs of the partnership which would dispose of the assets after you paid the debts of the partnership, and it was my opinion where there was outstanding contracts that those would be carried through to either their termination by delivery of the deed and closing out the property or by assignment in a dissolution.

130

Morrison: I direct your attention to Paragraphs 19A and B of the partnership agreement. That deals with the dissolution by the purchaser assets. Why at that time was it your opinion that that could not go forward?

White: It wasn't my opinion it couldn't go forward. It was my understanding it had not gone forward. There had not been a buy out of the limited partner by the general partner.

Morrison: Did you advise anyone not to go through with that buy out?

White: No.

Morrison: Did you advise anyone they should go through the terms of that buy out?

White: That I can't recall. I believe my response was to a specific question about who would step into the shoes of the general partner. I was not asked beyond that. I wasn't asked to interpret any provisions of the partnership agreement.

Morrison: Would it be your opinion that under the –are you familiar in nature and substance with the Uniform Limited Partnership Act?

White: I feel I am somewhat. I have not reviewed it in the last few months.

Morrison: Are you also familiar with the Uniform Partnership as opposed to the Limited Partnership?

White: Yes.

Morrison: Would you have an opinion or did you voice an opinion at that time as to why a limited partner, if he was the sole remaining partner, wouldn't be a surviving partner and thus have authority to wind up the North Carolina Uniform Partnership Act?

White: Right now it's hard to respond to that without pulling out the act and reading it. I have to refresh my memory as to what it says. I think one thing that influenced my opinion was that the partnership agreement itself provides that those negotiations for the buy out would be carried on by the personal representative of the deceased general partner.

Morrison: But the partnership agreement doesn't say that the executor of personal representative of the general partner will wind up the partnership though?

131

White:	Right.
Morrison:	It says the partnership will dissolve?
White:	Uh-huh.
Morrison:	Now, what steps would have been necessary at that time to dissolve and close up the partnership?
White:	Well, of course the procedure is set out in the statute. Generally, it involves a liquidation procedure whereby the debts of the partnership would be paid. Usually there is a provision for retaining of such funds to pay any debts that the partnership may have and liquidation or the distribution of the assets of the partnership.
Morrison:	Now, was it your understanding after these conversations between myself and you by phone and between the Mays that Mr. Neighbors ---was it your understanding that Mr. Jack Neighbors was going to stand in the stead of his deceased father with regard to winding up the partnership?
White:	Yes.
Morrison:	Did you advise him as to what would be necessary to wind up the partnership?
White:	I believe that I did. Again, I don't recall the specific conversation because I know I had several conversations with him, and exactly what I said I can't recall.
Morrison:	If you did so advise him would it have been through this series of conversations regarding what was to be done in these conversations with the Mays, you and he and myself?
White:	Yes, I believe it was.
Morrison:	To your knowledge what steps has he consulted you on with regard to winding up the partnership?
White:	Very little in that nature. I think sometime shortly after that I was aware or made aware that there was some disagreement between the Mays and Jack, and I recall telling him that because of my involvement in representing George and doing various closings and this sort of thing, he should have another attorney advise him about those matters because, technically, I would have been an attorney representing the partnership. And where the dispute arose

between the limited and general partner, I felt I might be in a conflicting situation.

Morrison: Can you remember when it was that you advised Mr. Neighbors that perhaps he should see another counsel?

White: I think shortly after he advised me of the agreement between he and Mr. Mays.

Morrison: Could this have been a few months just after George's death?

White: I believe it was. I don't think it was too long after that.

Morrison: After you so advised him, did he come back to you any time from then until now on for advice for handling the partnership affairs?

White: Not on that. Mostly all the conversations I've had with him since then related to matters which needed to be filed with the Clerk of Court in relation to the estate.

Morrison: Let me ask you, since George Neighbors' death or since July 25, 1983; have you made any payments from Neimay proceeds, from loans that you closed or any other Neimay money you may have had control of; have you made payments to any bank and the loan was not designated Neimay?

White: No, I don't believe I have. I don't recall that I have.

Morrison: Have you given any monies to Mr. Jack Neighbors from Neimay loan closing procedures or Neimay proceeds to pay any of his personal debts?

White: No.

Morrison: Have you given money to him from Neimay proceeds for him to personally deliver to the bank?

White: No. I think any check I have made from Neimay closings went from me – went from Neimay Limited Partnership on the check.

Morrison: Now, you explained earlier your procedure – excuse me, I have one other question before that.

	Were you aware of any construction loans taken out by Neimay or Neimay lending construction money or taking out any itself?
White:	Not that I recall. I have never been aware of any.
Morrison:	When you would be involved on behalf of Neimay for the real estate closing; that is, when a deed would be transferred from Neimay to the purchaser of the property, did you prepare a closing statement?
White:	If the funds went through my account, my trust account, I did. There were a number of closings where none of the purchase funds went through my account, and I was in the position of billing Neimay for my services and advancement to Neimay for generally the revenue stamps that went on the deed. If I received a check from the purchaser for a balance owed, then there would be a settlement statement but I wouldn't have a settlement statement for funds I never handled.
Morrison:	Was it frequent that you didn't handle funds in those closings?
White:	That was the rule.
Morrison:	Because of the installment land contract, and he would simply call you to prepare the deed?
White:	That's right.
Morrison:	Your office would be informed by documentation as to when the purchase price was received or received by Neighbors?
White:	I only had the word that it was paid by the general partnership. I believe from time to time occasionally there was some reimbursement to be made for taxes. I think the partnership contracts, installment contract, had a provision that the purchaser would be responsible for the real estate taxes, but of course, the contract not having gone through the county tax office there was never a transfer on the record so the property continued to be billed for tax purposes to Neimay which Neimay was making payments. And if any reimbursement was required, I remember from time to time being told that the purchaser owed so much on

134

back taxes. I can't separate in my mind how much of that occurred before or after George's death.

Morrison: Did you communicate to the deceased Mr. Neighbors and subsequently to his son that the partnership was paying taxes – did you communicate to the two Neighbors that the partnership was evidently paying taxes because of the unrecorded installment land contracts which they should not be obligated?

White: I don't recall that I communicated that to them. That's something they informed me, that taxes were due. They were aware taxes were being billed to Neimay.

Morrison: Would there be any reason for closing statements that you would submit to Neimay within those transactions to ever have been altered after they were transmitted to a purchaser or to the seller.

White: No, only unless there was an apparent correction that had to be made because of calculations, and the figures weren't correct on the statement. Sometimes someone using a calculator will make an error, and that happens after you add up the figures and they are not correct. You have to go back and make the corrections.

Morrison: Your settlement statement would reflect the date of closing?

White: Normally it's up in the upper right-hand corner.

Morrison: Now, I show you a letter – a copy of a letter written from you to Mr. Neighbors.

White: August 18, 1983.

Morrison: Is that, to your knowledge, an exact duplicate?

White: Yes, it seems to be a duplicate.

Morrison Do you recall the time of the writing of this letter?

White: Yes.

Morrison: Do you recall what prompted you to write this letter?

White: Yes. Obviously, there was a conversation that Danny Khoury had, a local attorney representing the purchaser of Lot 2 of Kitty Dunes Village and was in a position to close

135

and wanted clear deed to the lot, and that prompted me to write the letter because at that time I had no information that there was a pending closing.

This $5,000 hold back was pursuant to agreement we had with Safeco Title Insurance Company. They would issue a policy of title insurance to the purchaser on the existing contract without exception as to a lien or inheritance taxes. And that sum was held out of each closing to guarantee payment. The last paragraph was for the purpose of being able to supply the Internal Revenue Service with information. What I wanted to do, and I don't believe I ever got a chance to do it as I had the other estate that I had handled to which the decedent had a lot of real property which he had closings going on, in order to get a release from the Department of Revenue, you have to supply them with such information for them to ascertain there was sufficient assets to pay the state inheritance taxes. So I wanted to give them all of that information for that purpose so that we could get a release for the lots.

Once we had the release for the lots, any amounts held back could be released to Neimay.

Morrison: You used the expression in the first sentence, there is a comment of the "bind we find ourselves in." What exactly did you mean by that, or did you explain that?

White: Well, at the time I think I recall I had asked Jack to get me a copy of all outstanding contracts that George was involved in whether Neimay or anyone else so that I would know what lots – on what lots were outstanding contracts and I could better prepare myself to conduct closings on the existing contracts. In this situation I was contacted by an attorney who says "I'm ready for a deed and ready to close," and I had not been contacted by Jack or Kitty Dunes to say we have a contract paid out or a buyer on an existing contract, and we need to close; prepare the documents and here is the information. I didn't have that. In effect, Danny

	Khoury caught me cold as to my representation of the seller, and that's putting me in a bind.
Morrison:	So, you mean this $5,000 to be put aside is to satify the title company?
White:	That's right.
Morrison:	This is Neimay money?
White:	That would have been whatever partnership that closing occurred in. It would be those partnership funds, yes.
Morrison:	And this money was deposited into your trust account?
White:	I don't believe it was.
Morrison:	That wouldn't have gathered interest?
White:	No. Our anticipation was that it wouldn't be long. It would be a short period of time before they could be released.
Morrison:	That would ultimately go in George Neighbors' estate and to the limited partner, Mr. Mays; and then Mr. Mays was having proceeds diverted from his use without benefit of interest?
White:	Because the loan would be for the partnership property, until it was paid, there was no way I had of ascertaining the interest or the accounting other than to get a clear title to the purchaser to which the purchaser was entitled to receive from Neimay.
Morrison:	Whose idea was it to do that; was it yours or Mr. Jack Neighbors?
White:	If I recall it came out of the discussion I had with the title insurance company of what method we could use to go ahead and use the closing to go through and these people entitled to deeds to be able to receive their deeds.
Morrison:	So you advised Jack Neighbors of this process?
White:	Yes.
Morrison:	He was agreeable?
White:	Yes.
Morrison:	Were the Mays ever consulted on this?
White:	I didn't consult with them on it.

Morrison: Now, I'd like you to review – I want to show you some Photostats of what purports to be loan closings and loan procedures. First, let me show you what purports to be a note under date of June 23, 1983 in the amount of $40,000 to George and Dorothy T. Neighbors from Neimay at thirteen and a half percent interest. Do you know anything about that whatsoever?

White: No, I don't recall anything about that.

Morrison: All right. Now, I show you what purports to be a copy of a check that is numbered five eighty-nine drawn on Kitty Dunes Realty escrow account in the amount of $40,233.75 payable to the firm of Kellogg, White, Evans and Sharp under date of November 6, 1983. That would be your law firm's name?

White: That's right.

Morrison: And it's difficult to read, but I believe it says "Beasley closing."

White: That could be Beasley.

Morrison: I don't hold you to that. Let's look at that. Does this appear to be a closing statement prepared by your office?

White: Yes, it does.

Morrison: And would this be prepared under your direction or supervision?

White: Yes.

Morrison: It's under date of October 17, 1983; is that correct?

White: That's right.

Morrison: Would that have been the date of the transaction, the actual closing date?

White: Normally it would. Sometimes settlement statements are prepared ahead of time in anticipation and the closing may not occur on that date. But it's already drafted. Normally, that would be the date of closing and funds disbursed.

Morrison: It indicates balances are due to People's Bank and Trust, release price of $15, 075. That would be People's in Rocky Mount, and that's what they would be collecting for release of the purchase money deed of trust?

White: That's right.

Morrison:	There is a payment of $19,908.25 to Planters Bank, and then $5,000 withheld on the estate that we have just talked about?
White:	Right.
Morrison:	Okay. Now, turning over I show you what purports to be a copy of Check Number 9757 drawn on your law firm's account in the amount of $19,908.25 that being the amount identical to the payoff to Planters Bank, and the check is further Neimay Limited Partnership designation as what the check is, and it appears also, "Beasley", at the top.
White:	Yeah.
Morrison:	Would this be the check paying off a Neimay loan from Beasley proceeds?
White:	That would be my understanding of it, and I probably received that direction.
Morrison:	The check also appears to be negotiated by the bank on November 14 of 1983. Can you tell me what would be the reason for having money like $20,000 from an October 17, 1983 closing not transmitted to the bank until – not being negotiated by the bank until November?
White:	Apparently the check was written approximately seven days after the closing date, unless the closing did not occur on that date and was a few day later. The date of the check is the 24th of October, 1983. The check was written – the settlement date on the statement was October 17. There was a period of seven days difference, and I can't account for the seven days other than the possibility that it closed later than the original anticipated closing date, and I had been prepared; but it appears it was negotiated November 14. I couldn't explain it. I can't tell you what it is. I can get a fourteen out of that. It looks like ND, and some letters that aren't readable.
Morrison:	Now I show you another closing statement that appears to be Howard Olds' property, Lot Number 2, Kitty Dunes under date of August 22, 1983. Would this have been prepared under your direction?
White:	Yes.

Morrison:	Now, at the bottom you have written, "Planters National Bank to be applied on note per Jack, 11-14-83" and you are talking about $3,573.30; do you recall what that would mean?
White:	Other than Jack would have contacted either me or my secretary to inform me that payment was due Planters in that amount of this closing.
Morrison:	That was August 22?
White:	I can't be sure of the date of closing unless I looked at the date of the deed itself, the date it was recorded which would reflect the date of the actual closing.
Morrison:	It might have been your procedure that documents might have been prepared in August and the matter not close until later?
White:	Quite often that can happen. It is not unusual for closing to get delayed for a month or so, and this could have been into the time that we were negotiating the release prices. What had to be held back because of the estate, I'm not sure.
Morrison:	We have a closing date of 8-22, and you are saying to be applied to note per Jack, 11-14-83. Why would you know on August 22 what Jack wanted done on 11-14-83?
White:	I don't know, and I don't know whether the date 11-14-83 is a date the payment was to be made or the date he informed me and it was put there. The date that the settlement statement was actually made. I can't say without going through the files.
Morrison:	It appears that we have three closing statements here on Howard W. Olds, Jr. They all appear to be for the same lot and under the same date yet there are differences. Could you explain those differences?
White:	I assume these are ones I gave you out of my files?
Morrison:	If I may show you what we are dealing with here.
White:	I don't see any differences with the figures. I see differences in the writing.
Morrison:	Whose writing?

White: That's my writing there, and apparently, that was typed
           from this copy of that. The fourteen may be a mistake, and
           it should have been a one.

Morrison: That is your writing on the closing statement, the writing
           we're talking about, the payment to Planters National Bank
           and transmit to Jack Neighbors. All right. Now, what would
           that mean, payable to Planters?

White: I was instructed to make payment to Planters but send it to
           him to make the payment.

Morrison: Who instructed you to do that?

White: Jack Neighbors would be the only one.

Morrison: Would this be a check made to Planters Bank but not
           indicated what it was to be made payable for?

White: That's possible.

Morrison: But it was Neimay money?

White: That's right.

Morrison: Why would there be – why wouldn't it be more customary
           to mail the check to Planters rather to Jack?

White: I was responding to the direction of the person who
           normally gave me directions in doing the closing.

Morrison: On earlier closing statement in this file I have in front of
           you, under the same date a typed closing statement that
           indicates that the balance is to go to Planters National Bank
           applied on note per Jack. However, on the one we just
           reviewed, it indicates that the balance is payable to Neimay
           Partnership.

White: Unless between the time I had prepared this and he had
           given me information I received a phone call to do it
           differently, which could have been possible.

Morrison: That call would have come from Jack Neighbors?

White: Uh-huh.

Morrison: Can you think why it would be altered to do it that way?

White: No, I didn't normally question it. You know, if I had
           instructions to begin with to make it payable to Planters,
           apparently after I had typed this up and received subsequent
           instructions rather than sending it straight to the bank, then

	I would have complied and that would account for the change.
Morrison:	Were any of these whited out to reflect this; the secretarial process of taking white-out?
White:	Without looking at the original, I couldn't tell you.
Morrison:	Would you be in possession of the original?
White:	Normally they would have been sent to Neighbors. It goes to the seller.
Morrison:	This appears to be a check drawn on your law firm at 9879, and it is in the amount of $3,573.30 which appears to be the amounts that were proceeds going to Neimay Partnership on Howard Olds' Lot 2, Kitty Dunes. Again, making reference of the closing date appearing to be August 22, 1983, and your check is not made out until November 14, 1983 and not negotiated until November 16, 1983. Do you know what the reason would be for the discrepancy or difference in the closing statement and the check?
White:	Other than I was told not to send the check to the bank until a certain date.
Morrison:	Why would that be? What reason would there be for you to hold money for almost four months?
White:	I don't know. I don't know.
Morrison:	If there was a Neimay obligation at the bank, and if you had Neimay proceeds in your trust account which does not generate interest; that is correct?
White:	That's right.
Morrison:	Then by the holding of this money, there would be interest accruing on the Neimay obligation which would have been reduced by prompt payment, would it not?
White:	Right.
Morrison:	And you can't recall any reason?
White:	I can't recall any reason other than – unless I had some idea of the time frame when we were trying to work out some method to be able to convey the property without the lien of inheritance taxes. That's the only thing I can think of because I couldn't convey clear title until some arrangements had been made.

Well, to clarify, I need to see what dates the deeds were recorded and look and see what period of time I was negotiating with the title insurance company to try to work out a method by which we could take care of that.

There have been instances, and I can't recall whether in relation to this estate without going back and looking, whereby the seller or buyer and seller agreed that I could go ahead and record the deed but not disburse the money until some arrangment had been made to clear the lien.

Morrison;   I show you what purports to be a closing statement of October 25, 1983 prepared under your letterhead recording John Ryder. Look at that, please, and see if it was prepared under your instructions.

White: Yes.

Morrison: It indicates a closing date of October 25, 1983 and indicates $3,000.53 is to be applied on note per instructions of Jack Neighbors. That $3,000.53 would be Neimay money?

White: Right.

Morrison: Do you know what note it would be applied to.

White: No.

Morrison: Do you recall anything about whether you gave any note directly to Jack Neighbors or sent it to the bank?

White: I couldn't say.

Morrison: Again, let me ask you to review what appears to be your Check Number 9922 drawn on your account for $3,000.53 payable to Planters Bank. It appears to be under date of November 21, 1983, approximately a month – not quite a month – after what appears to be the closing.

Do you know of any reason why there would be that lapse in time?

White: Other than the same reason, I couldn't disburse with buyer and seller until we worked out the release.

143

Morrison:	I have a closing statement of February 7 for A. Wayne Anderson and wife, Lot 19, Kitty Dunes. Was that made under your instructions and supervision?
White:	Yes.
Morrison:	This indicates a balance of $768 was to go to John B. Neighbors, executor. Wouldn't that have been payable to the Neimay Partnership?
White:	Yes, it should have been.
Morrison:	Do you know why it was made payable to Mr. Neighbors directly?
White:	Assuming these funds came from Neimay, then that should go to the Neimay account.
Morrison:	Do you know of any reason to assume that the funds didn't come from Neimay?
White:	No, other than that statement. That's the only inference.
Morrison:	Do you remember anything independently about this?
White:	No, I don't.
Morrison:	This last one, Mr. White, is Stanley B. Barger, under date of February 29, 1984. Do you recall this transaction?
White:	I don't have any independent recollection.
Morrison:	Do you recall any discussion about this property not being sold?
White:	No.
Morrison:	These pieces I have shown you, these closing statements, are after Mr. Neighbors' death. Do you know if these pieces of property were under contract before his death, or was this new business going on?
White:	As I recall most of the contracts were contracts that had been executed prior to George's death. I understand there was a point that there was some distribution of lots between Jack and the Mays, and I do recall some conversation with Jack about one or more closings that had been entered into afterward where it was okay for both parties to go ahead and close them.
Morrison:	Let me show you this other writing that appears to be scribbled.

"Two certificates to Ray White, assignment P, plus one fixed thirteen percent" on one page, and on the page prior to that number, "Kellogg, Tom White, note for Beasley." Do you have any familiarity about this document at all?

White: I don't believe I've ever seen it.

Morrison: Do you recognize the handwriting?

White: No, I don't.

Morrison: Okay. Just a moment, please. One last question, Mr. White. Do you know of any Neimay money being misappropriated or diverted from the Mays?

White: No, I don't. I never had access to nor was I ever involved in any of the accounting of any of the Neimay funds other than what would have come through me in relation to a closing.

Morrison: Thank you. I don't have any other questions.

BY MR. ABBOTT

Abbott: Is it your testimony that the reason you put $5,000, supposedly Neimay funds, into your trust escrow account was because that is the way the insurance company required you to do before they would insure the property being purchased?

White: That's correct. There was a hold harmless indemnity arrangement worked out with the title insurance company which the seller, Neimay, through Jack Neighbors agreed to hold the title insurance company harmless and indemnify the company for any lien being exerted by the state or Internal Revenue Service, and part of that was holding that much money until such time they were satisfied it could be released.

Abbott: Is that unusual?

White: No, it's been done numerous times before.

Abbott: All right. Now, approximately how long did you retain that money in your trust account that you can recall?

White: That's very difficult to say. It was held until, I believe, the inheritance tax returns were prepared.

145

Analysis by author

When Tom White was asked by John Morrison what steps had Jack Neighbors consulted him on with regard to winding up the partnership - he replied ---"Very little in that nature. I think sometime shortly after that I was aware or made aware that there was some disagreement between the Mays and Jack, and I recall telling him that because of my involvement in representing George and doing various closings and this sort of thing, he should have another attorney advise him about those matters because, technically, I would have been an attorney representing the partnership. And where the dispute arose between the *limited* and *general partner*, I felt I might be in a conflicting situation."

Mr. White first denied taking any Neimay money out of closings and paying it to Planters National Bank on any loan that wasn't Neimay. He further denied giving Neimay money to Jack Neighbors to be applied on a Planters National Bank that wasn't Neimay.

According to his settlement statements, he did both.

Chris Payne, Planters National Bank, under oath twice, clearly states that the $40,000 note is a personal note of George Neighbors. He clearly states, under oath, that the bank would look to the estate for payment.

Jack Adams, the Neimay CPA, clearly states, under oath, that Peoples Bank was paid in full on June 23, 1983 for the $400,000 mortgage owed. He included that in his accounting that was required by the court. After that, three payments were held out of Tom White's closings that designated they were *for release to Peoples*. Since the mortgage had already been paid off, Jack Adams *treated* these amounts falsely as "loans to George Neighbors" on his court required accounting. Where did the "actual" money go? It did not go through a Neimay account.

This was an accounting lawsuit and a big part of it included false Neimay loans to George Neighbors.

It appears from Mr. White's testimony, both in deposition and trial transcript, that he acted in the interest of Planters National Bank and the estate of George Neighbors and not in the interest of the *limited partner*.

Regarding the question directed by O. C. Abbott, about the $5,000 being held in Mr. White's trust escrow account for the insurance company so they would insure the property being purchased, Mr. White said "Neimay, through Jack Neighbors, agreed to hold the title insurance company harmless and indemnify the company for any lien being exerted by the state or Internal Revenue Service."

Jack Neighbors didn't have that legal right. His attorney and Tom White both knew it.

We were told that all of the deeds passed after George's death of July 23, 1983 needed the signature of the *limited partner* in order to be clear. There are at least sixteen deeds out there in Dare County that don't meet this requirement.

Debbie J. Burgess, Johnson and Burgess Company, Neimay accountants is fifth up second day.

The following is taken from trial transcript of February 19, 1991.

Morrison:	Have you worked on any Neimay Limited Partnership accounts since 1985?
Burgess:	Yes.
Morrison:	In what capacity?
Burgess:	As their CPA.
Morrison:	So you have served since 1985. You have been the partnership accountant to Neimay partnership?
Burgess:	Actually since February 15, 1986.
Morrison:	Are you the personal accountant of Jack Neighbors?
Burgess:	Yes, sir.
Morrison:	And you became responsible for the Neimay accounting in 1986; is that what you said?
Burgess:	February 15, 1986.

Morrison: And you were retained by Mr. Neighbors to do that?
Burgess: Yes.
The Court: Fifteenth of 86?
Burgess: Yes, sir.
Morrison: Now, ma'am, since that time, have you retained the services of Mr. Jack Adams, who earlier testified, to assist you or work with you in any way on any Neimay accountings?
Burgess: No, not that I can recall.
Morrison: Have you paid any monies to Mr. Adams for preparation of anything regarding Neimay?
Burgess: No.

Morrison: Okay. Now, do you recall a time when pursuant to court ordered discovery, Mr. Hollowell and Ms. Mays came to your office to examine this file?
Burgess: Yes. But this isn't all of it.
Morrison: This is not all of it?
Burgess: No. This is only the stuff Jack did up through '85.
Morrison: Was everything that's in this file available to Mr. Hollowell when they came to your office?
Burgess: I don't know because I am not exactly sure what's in that box. That box is not really a file. I am not sure what's in there.
Morrison: So but you turned over to them everything that you had at that time?
Burgess: No, sir.
Morrison: You did not?
Burgess: Not everything, huh-uh.
Morrison: You did not turn over everything you had regarding the Neimay partnership?
Burgess: Under the terms of the court order, I turned over everything that I had for the Neimay partnership that was based on the --- that had anything to do with the original accountings or filings of tax returns or financial statements.
Morrison: I ask you in particular if this accounting was in the file?

148

Burgess:	No.
Morrison:	It was not?
Burgess:	No.
Morrison:	And I ask you in particular if these supplementary documents were in the file?
Burgess:	No.
Morrison:	And if this was in the file.
ABBOTT:	May I inquire?
The Court:	He's talking about the things that were added, the things that Mr. Adams said he prepared just recently.
ABBOTT:	No, sir. I think he's talking about something else besides that.
The Court:	Well, I didn't think so.
Morrison:	No.
ABBOTT:	The first piece of paper.
Burgess:	I am assuming you are talking about the things that are attached to that account.
Morrison:	We are talking about ---let's take the accounting first.
Burgess:	Right, that was not in there.
Morrison:	That was not in there. What was the purpose of the Neimay accounting not being in the Neimay papers?
Burgess:	Because the court order, you know --- I mean I had an adversary walking in saying, "I want to see all of your files." The files belong to us, not to the partnership. The court order said to provide all of the records that pertained to the accounting for Neimay. That did not pertain to the original accounting of Neimay. That was prepared from the original accounting. I provided every annual accounting that was ever prepared for Neimay.
Morrison:	You prepared every single annual accounting?
Burgess:	I provided every accounting that was ever prepared for Neimay.
Morrison:	But this one that was prepared by Mr. Adams and tendered as an accounting was not in the file?
Burgess:	No.

Morrison: Now, ma'am, you, despite the court order – you said you
              are the partnership accountant?
Burgess: Yes.
Morrison: Now the partnership consists of Mr. Mays and Mr.
              Neighbors?
Burgess: Right.
Morrison: But you said this was an adversarial proceeding as far as
              you were ---
Burgess: Well, I knew they were in a lawsuit.
Morrison: But they were not adverse to you.
Burgess: No, no, no.
Morrison: Now was there any reason that you did not want them to
              see these other records?
Burgess: It's not that I did not want them to see them, it's that I
              felt that it was my responsibility and duty to only turn
              over the things that were strictly called for by the court. I
              wasn't going to just hand them my file and say, "Here, look
              through it." I went through and pulled out the things that
              were specifically asked for by the court and gave them to
              them.
Morrison: But you understood that Mr. Hollowell was acting as agent
              of Mr. Mays?
Burgess: Yes.
Morrison   Okay. Now, you said that these are your work papers..
Burgess: Yes.
Morrison: This is your file. It does not belong to the client?
Burgess: No, sir.
Morrison: Do you recognize the code of Professional Ethics for
              the American Institute of Certified Public Accountants
              and the North Carolina State Society of Certified Public
              Accountants as setting forth the ethics of your profession?
Burgess: Yes, sir.
Morrison: And is it customary to follow those ethics?
Burgess: Yes, sir.
Morrison: And are you familiar with Rule 501, Acts Discreditable to
              the Profession?

Burgess: If it's in there I've read it at some point in time. I don't
             know it by number.
Morrison: You might want to review that.

Morrison: Under previous – you are aware that there was a
             distribution of certain installment contracts between the
             parties?
Burgess: I was aware – from what I was told, my understanding
             is that the contracts themselves were never actually
             distributed, could not be distributed.
Morrison: Who told you that they were never actually distributed?
Burgess: Mr. Neighbors.
Morrison: He said they had never been assigned to Mr. and Mrs.
             Mays?
Burgess: He said they couldn't be legally assigned.
Morrison: Mr. Neighbors told you that they had not been distributed.
Burgess: Right, not legally, the contracts themselves.
Morrison: So all tax returns that you have prepared since any
             divisions of accounts, if they were, indicate taxable income
             to the partnership?
Burgess: Yes, sir.
Morrison: And wouldn't this also not cause the duplication of tax on
             individuals?
Burgess: Not that I know of.
Morrison: Well, isn't – can you tell us what a K-1 is?
Burgess: A K-1 is a schedule that's attached to the partnership tax
             return which is provided to the individual partners to give
             them the information from the partnership tax return to file
             their individual tax returns.
Morrison: Thank you, ma'am.

CROSS EXAMINATION BY MR. ABBOTT

Abbott: Ms. Burgess, a partnership doesn't pay taxes, do they?
Burgess: No, sir.

Abbott:	Now, do you know whether or not that Mr. Mays and Mr. Morrison have already been furnished that form that he put out to you that you said you took out of the file?
Burgess:	Yes, sir. You had told me that he had already had that and Mr. Neighbors had told me.
Abbott:	And the fact that it was attached to Mr. Adams' deposition, was that not done?
Burgess:	I never saw Mr. Adams' deposition.
Abbott:	And you furnished to them also a total computerized listing from 1975 right on through 1988, did you not, or 1985. What was it that you furnished them?
Burgess:	What we attempted to do was an accounting, a restatement of the accounting, from '85 to '88 probably.
Abbott:	Every transaction that had – everything that happened?
Burgess:	Yes.
Abbott:	And you did it on a computer basis?
Burgess:	Right.
Abbott:	And they didn't like that.
Burgess:	Obviously not.
Abbott:	Now you said you have not done a 1989 tax return. Do you know whether or not there's any business been done by Neimay partnership?
Burgess:	I don't know. I have not seen the checkbook.
Abbott:	Thank you, ma'am.
The Court:	That's all.

Analysis by author

First, Debbie Burgess states, under oath, that she had been the Neimay Partnership accountant since February 15, 1986. She was aware that the partnership consists of Mr. Mays and Mr. Neighbors. She further stated that at the same time she was accountant for Jack Neighbors, personally. She also appeared to be accountant for the estate.

It appears that Ms. Burgess was ill informed by Jack Neighbors and his attorney O. C. Abbott about several matters. Jack Adams' deposition of July 10, 1986 should have been given to her. Jack Adams and Jack Neighbors should have kept her more informed of current events. She was performing accounting without the proper documentation. She was acting on their word.

Ms. Burgess made reference, under oath, that Jack Neighbors told her the installment contracts and the lots that were split between him and Ms. Mays were not legal. She said, under oath, that Jack Neighbors told her they couldn't be legally assigned. Tom White evidently didn't have the same opinion because he legally spit them. *She got more bad advice.* She never checked with the Mays or their accountant about the lots. The plaintiff's agent sold all of those lots and they were closed properly with all necessary signatures. Debbie Burgess chose to believe Jack Neighbors, without even asking the Mays or their accountant any questions. She filled out the partnership returns as if the lots had never been split. That presented a double taxation for the Mays.

Ms. Burgess testified that Jack Adams had not performed any Neimay business or other business for them since 1985. In November of 1988, an adjustment was entered into the estate of George Neighbors that was on the letterhead of Johnson and Burgess Company. It was signed by Debbie J. Burgess and initialed by JA. It was an adjustment for the second "hidden" estate account that had been discovered by the *limited partner* in September of 1988. The hidden estate account involved a partnership by George Neighbors and Jack Adams called Kitty Dunes Height. The adjustment – on Johnson and Burgess letterhead was for 1983, 1984, 1985, 1986, and 1987. It was presented to the Clerk of Court on November 10, 1988. It affected the estate.

Ms. Burgess testified, under oath, that she was aware of the Neimay lawsuit. In that respect, she should have understood the lawsuit was against Jack Neighbors personally as well as the estate of his father.

Douglas A. Hollowell, CPA for the Limited Partner is sixth up second day.

The following is taken from the trial transcript of February 19, 1991.

Mr. Hollowell testified to his educational background and the many real estate projects in which he had been involved. In addition, the following was testified to:

Morrison:	And you have qualified as an expert witness in accounting in the courts of North Carolina and Virginia before, have you not?
Hollowell:	That is correct.
Morrison:	So I believe you've also served on the Virginia State Bar on the Ethics Committee.
Hollowell:	Yes. I was a layperson for the Fourth District Committee of the Virginia State Bar Association for two years.

Morrison:	Now, based upon your examination of the documents that have been furnished regarding an accounting, do you have an opinion as to whether or not they are in fact an accounting within the meaning of your profession?
ABBOTT;	Objection
The Court:	Overruled.
Hollowell:	The accounting documents that Ms. Mays and Mr. Mays were supplied with in 1985, I believe, for the ten year periods, there is no way looking at those documents to determine what the assets and liabilities are at a particular point in time, which is what this whole matter is about.
Morrison:	Would you explain why?
Hollowell:	The worksheets that we as accountants work with, Mr. Adams alluded to, they are the basis upon which we make adjustments to these transactions that Mr. Adams has taken the time to go back and reconstruct from the original documents. Okay. And this is the point that I think Ms. Burgess was a little confused on.
ABBOTT:	Objection
The Court:	Overruled.
Hollowell:	These records that we are talking about are not the accountant's records. We merely, in what has been

154

described as "Write up work," we really serve as a conduit for the bookkeeper that would normally be hired and retained by any client that comes to us for accounting services.

Those records, even though we paid for the materials – we paid for the pencils, the paper clips, whatever – they belong to the client. The American Institute of CPAs and the North Carolina Society, Virginia Society, are all very clear on these points. We may copy those records and keep copies, but they belong to the client. They are not ours. That's clear.

Morrison: I understand. All right. But my question is can you tell us what is irregular, if irregular, if anything, about the tendered accounting?

Hollowell: That they do not give a balance sheet at a point in time. At the end of a year, normally, is when an accounting cycle will terminate. For tax purposes we have to report on a 12 month period, except in the first and last year of an organization's existence. So there was no attempt in these documents to define what the assets or the liabilities were.

The thing that puzzles me about all of this information is why Mr. Adams would have his original cash receipts and disbursement, his adjusting entries, and his worksheets already in his files, but yet take the time to come back and copy over these transactions, which in many cases still don't foot to the original documents. I cannot understand why anyone would want to do that. Even if I was taking one of the lowest paid staff members, why would I want to waste time doing that? Why not just copy the original documents which belong to the client anyway? That's what puzzles me.

Morrison: I see. Do you have an opinion as an accountant whether the documents tendered accurately reflect the partnership transactions based on what you have seen?

Hollowell:	We have not been obviously prepared an audit. The transaction could be easily verified to bank reconciliations, but – I am not sure I quite understand your question. But whether they've been transcribed as in the original documents, we ultimately obtained after five years effort, we haven't gone – we've tested some of them. They appeared to be okay. But it's still difficult to determine and impossible from what we received and used for five years to determine what the assets were.
Morrison:	In making an accounting, is it customary to document loans within a partnership without any existing legal memorandum?
Hollowell:	I would say it's typically – we would want that documentation in our file. In many cases clients need to be instructed as to the need for these documents. If there were partnership advances or officer loans being taken out, we need to communicate to our clients that there needs to be evidence of an obligation in order to stay away from constructive dividends if nothing else. And there needs to be at least an annual accrual of interest on those obligations whether it's paid or not.
Morrison:	Would you define the accounting term "Single entity?"
The Court:	What did you ask him?
Morrison:	To define the accounting term "Single entity."
ABBOTT:	Objection, Your Honor.
The Court:	Single what?
Morrison:	Entity.
ABBOTT:	Objection.
The Court:	I don't know what you mean by that, but I will let him answer.
Hollowell:	The single entity concept is one of the basic accounting principles that we are taught in an entry-level accounting course, first chapter. That is that all accounting matters related to that particular entity will be transacted through that entity, that there will be no co-mingling and no other transactions that will occur – very simple accounting basic entry level course.

Morrison:	From the testimony you have heard and the documents you have studied with regard to this case, has that principle been followed in making this accounting?
Hollowell:	It certainly does not appear to be.
Morrison:	Is that a substantial or a minor violation of performing an accounting?
ABBOTT:	Objection, Your Honor.
The Court:	Overruled.
Hollowell:	When you find co-mingling and you find it to the extent that we have seen here, it leads to greater questions as to propriety of all the transactions that were occurring. How far do you have to expand your test? If we were doing an audit, you would be talking about considerable fees. Of course, that was not an audit. But the same caution needs to be exerted when we are preparing any type of accounting in today's litigation society. So we need to be careful that all the transactions are there.
Morrison:	Thank you.

Analysis by author

We simply did not get the proper records or accounting in order to determine the assets and liability of the Neimay Limited Partnership. There was a deliberate stall on the part of the executor, the lawyer, the bankers and the accountants from 1983 to 1991. It was impossible to determine the assets and liabilities.

<u>Chris Payne, Vice President, Planters National Bank, Outer Banks is seventh up second day.</u>

The following is from the trial transcript of February 19, 1991

Morrison:	Would you give us your name, please?
Payne:	Chris Payne
The Court:	How do you spell your lasts name?
Payne:	P-a-y-n-e
Morrison:	And where do you live, Mr. Payne?
Payne:	I live in Colington Harbour.

Morrison:	And that's here in Dare County?
Payne:	Yes, sir.
Morrison:	And how are you employed, sir?
Payne:	I am a senior vice president with Centura Bank successor by merger to Planters National Bank.
Morrison:	And how long have you been so employed?
Payne:	Since July 3rd, 1969.

In Mr. Payne's deposition dated September 12, 1986, he was asked by John Morrison why the Beasley $40,233.75 Neimay check would have been taken out of the Neimay account.

Morrison:	But at any rate, this indicates that it was deposited in error on July 12, 1983, and it is therefore taken out of the Neimay account and put in the Kitty Dunes Account?
Payne:	That's what it looks like.
Morrison:	Who would have the authority to advise Ms. Austin to do that? Can she do that on her own?
Payne:	No. Generally speaking, someone connected with the estate or someone who is authorized to withdraw checks for someone connected with the estate or someone ---
Morrison:	Where is the estate in this? We are not talking estate here, are we?
Payne:	No, but you asked me who could withdraw on the Neimay Limited account and if Neimay had estate authority or the partnership had estate authority and that partner had the same authority as if the person were not deceased then. The person depositing the money or his agent could order this money be taken out, or anyone assigned on the Neimay Limited account.
Morrison:	How could we ascertain who gave Ms. Austin this authority?
Payne:	Other than asking her and if she remembered.
Morrison:	Would she have to seek authority from anyone else in the bank?

Payne:	No.
Morrison:	She could do this entirely on her own?
Payne:	Right.

Under oath, Chris Payne, referring to the $40,000 note, testified that it was a personal note of George Neighbors and if anything happened to him, the bank would look to the estate for payment.

Analysis by author
O. C. Abbott had established in the very beginning of this lawsuit, that Jack Neighbors had no connection to the Neimay Partnership. Therefore, he had no legal right to withdraw Neimay money from the Neimay account. Jack Neighbors had no legal right to make *any* Neimay decisions. Jack Neighbors was well aware of that.

W. Ray White, President, Planters National Bank, Manteo is eighth up second day.

Mr. White was not deposed for deposition in 1986.
The following is taken from the trial transcript on February 19, 1991.

Morrison:	Give us your name please, sir.
White:	Ray White
Morrison:	And where do you live, Mr. White?
White:	Nags Head.
Morrison:	How are you employed, sir?
White:	Centura Bank.
Morrison:	And in what capacity are you employed with Centura Bank?
White:	I am the area executive for the Outer Banks.
Morrison:	And how long have you been so ----- this is, of course, as just testified, the successor to Planters?
White:	Yes.
The Court:	Were you at Planters?
White:	Yes, sir.
Morrison:	How long have you been so employed?

White: I have been with Planters for 24 years. And I've been in this particular position probably close to ten.

During the rest of the testimony, Mr. Ray White either didn't remember or couldn't recall most of what was asked of him.

Analysis by author
Very little. He was president of Planters National Bank. During this time, he was a partner in a real estate development called Sea Ventures Company with Norman W. Shearin, Jr., Thomas L. White, Jr. and James F. Perry, an Outer Banks realtor. *I don't know whether this presents a conflict of interest or not.* At the same time of Sea Ventures, Mr. Shearin and Mr. White were also involved with the Neimay Partnership.

Shirley Mays, Plaintiff's Agent, is last witness up second day and only witness up third day – except for recalls

I, Shirley Mays, was the last witness up. I was on the stand six hours the first day and three hours the next. John Morrison put 31 exhibits in the record with extensive explanation from me. The defendant's attorney offered no exhibits.

I want to mention this. Two of our most prominent attorneys in the area sat through the entire three-day trial. One was from Elizabeth City, that same good friend of mine and one was from Manteo. They were our only audience and I wondered why they stayed the entire three days. They didn't sit out in the audience. They sat behind the defendant and his group – as if they were supporting them.

The Dare County Register of Deeds later told me that the one from Manteo was a good friend of the visiting judge.

I didn't realize until 1996 – five years after this trial - that I had been at the tip of an iceberg.

Neimay was a little white-collar crime compared to the one going on at the same time across town in Manteo – just a few blocks away. The Great Atlantic S&L robbery was a much bigger real estate scam. The Great Atlantic went defunct with 747 other S&L Institutions in the country and at that very moment in 1991 prime Outer Banks properties were being "mishandled" at a very fast pace. Some of the lawyers involved in the Neimay closings were very active in closings at that Manteo S&L.

We presented a lot of evidence during the trial that should have been extremely damaging to Tom White, Jack Adams and Planters Bank. I still believe that Jack Neighbors was the least guilty. But I do realize that this almost eight-year obstruction of justice could not have been pulled off without him

The evidence presented was overwhelming. It is all a matter of record.

I do feel compelled to tell you about this one very blatant example of commingling that I presented in court to Judge George Fountain. As I told you Jeffrey disappeared off the Coast of Cape Hatteras on November 13, 1980 at 1:30 p.m. never to be seen again. At the time of his disappearance, there was international drug dealing going on and it was reported in the local paper that their base was the Oregon Inlet Fishing Center. *This is all a matter of public record.* That is a central docking area for the deep-sea charter boats. It is also very near a Coast Guard facility. Several of the local Coast Guardsmen were related to the local fishermen. Unfortunately, a lot of local fishermen got involved in the drug dealing in the early 80's. Several were indicted and many have never been caught. *They know who they are.*

Lunsford Crew, Jr., an Outer Bank resident was a local captain who piloted a receiver-ship through local channels between December of 1978 and spring of 1981. He was indicted for drug dealing. One of George Neighbors' discovered accounts, which had Neimay funds commingled throughout, dealt with a closing between Lunsford Crew's personal property and George Neighbors.

Lunsford Crew, Sr. (Lunsford's father) prepared the deed. After being recorded, it was sent to Tom White. Tom White personally drew up the deed of trust and had it sent back to him. The very same day of filing – May 19, 1991 - and written from the same account, were three checks –two to Kellogg attorneys and one to Planters National Bank for $9,548.08. The big check for just under $10,000 was turned into a certified check by someone at Planters and noted *DO NOT RETURN*. They were all signed by George Neighbors. Please note that the big check, just under $10,000 which was turned into a cashiers check "clearly" states that it is to Kellogg – White Evans for the Crew closing. *It peaked my interest because Neimay funds were commingled in that account.*

Pay to the order of
PLANTERS NATIONAL BANK
FOR DEPOSIT ONLY
KELLOGG, WHITE, EVANS & SHARP
TRUST ACCOUNT

MAY 20 '61

PAY ANY BK. OR BKR., P.E.G.
THE PLANTERS NATIONAL BANK

Pay to the Order Of
PLANTERS NATIONAL BANK
FOR DEPOSIT ONLY
KELLOGG, WHITE, EVANS & SHARP
TRUST ACCOUNT

MAY 20 '61

PAY ANY BK. OR BKR., P.E.G.
THE PLANTERS NATIONAL BANK

DO NOT RETURN
CASHIER'S CHECK ISSUED IN LIEU OF

PAY ANY BK. OR BKR., P.E.G.
THE PLANTERS NATIONAL BANK

G. W. NEIGHBORS
OR JOHN B. NEIGHBORS
BOX 275
KITTY HAWK, N.C. 27949

2933

66-85
531

5--18 1981

PAY TO THE ORDER OF Starky Sharp $241 48

Two Hundred Forty One & 48 — DOLLARS

PLANTERS NATIONAL BANK
AND TRUST COMPANY
NAGS HEAD, N.C. 27959

FOR May Pay - Bal

⑆0000 2933⑆ ⑈053 1008 50⑉90⑈3 146 278⑈ ⑆0000 24 148⑆

G. W. NEIGHBORS
OR JOHN B. NEIGHBORS
BOX 275
KITTY HAWK, N.C. 27949

2932

66-85
531

5-19 1981

PAY TO THE ORDER OF Tom White $1164 50

Eleven Hundred Sixty Four & 50 — DOLLARS

PLANTERS NATIONAL BANK
AND TRUST COMPANY
NAGS HEAD, N.C. 27959

FOR

⑆0000 2932⑆ ⑈053 1008 50⑉90⑈3 146 278⑈ ⑆0000 116450⑆

G. W. NEIGHBORS
OR JOHN B. NEIGHBORS
BOX 275
KITTY HAWK, N.C. 27949

2931

66-85
531

5-19 1981

PAY TO THE ORDER OF PNB

DO NOT RETURN

KITTY DUNES 9548 DOLS 08 CTS — DOLLARS

CASHIER'S CHECK ISSUED IN LIEU OF

PLANTERS NATIONAL BANK
AND TRUST COMPANY
NAGS HEAD, N.C. 27959

Crew

FOR Cashiers check for Kellogg - Whit Crew

⑆0000 2931⑆ ⑈053 1008 50⑉90⑈3 146 278⑈ ⑆0000954808⑆

When I mentioned Lunsford Crew's name in court while testifying, Judge Fountain turned his head sharply and said to me "Whom did you say?" "I said Lunsford Crew, your Honor. His father is a well known attorney in Roanoke Rapids." He said, "I know his father. He's a friend of mine."

I immediately knew that I had not made any points with Judge George Fountain. I thought the discovery was important because our partnership money was commingled in that account and it was NOT a Neimay account. I'm not sure he heard anything I said after that.

This same account of George's – with Neimay money going through it – had a couple of Nunemaker Wholesale checks that worried me a lot. George had sold my husband *Nunemaker Retail* and Charles Nunemaker and his wife kept *Nunemaker Wholesale*. We were unaware of the close friendship between Charles Nunemaker's current wife and George Neighbors or any fishy business that they were conducting together.

The same account that held Lunsford Crew money held another couple of checks that I questioned. One was from a seafood company in St. Petersburg, Florida and made out to *Nunemaker Wholesale Fish Co* for $11,753.00. It went directly into that account even though it was made out to *Nunemaker Wholesale Fish Co*. There was another check from Harriet Nunemaker (Charles' first wife) to George for $1,747.00. Together, they totaled $13,500 – all dated the same day. REMEMBER, we did not own Nunemaker WHOLESALE. Again, I did not know that George Neighbors was in the fish business. *Again, I was mostly concerned because Neimay money was going in and out of that account.*

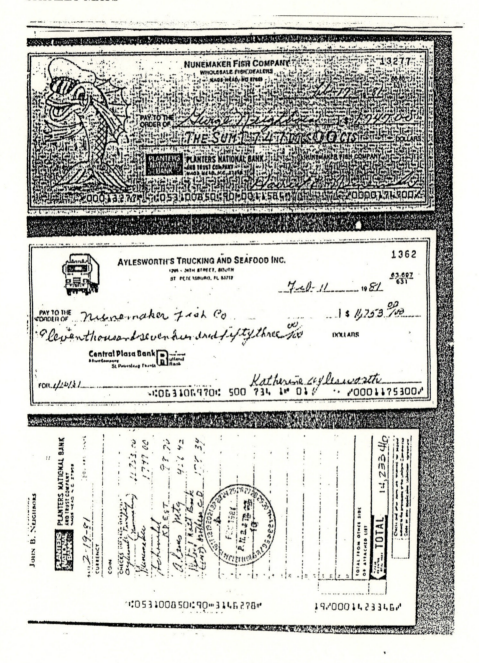

The same account had a lot of checks for guns. I did not know that George Neighbors was a gun collector. *I was only concerned about the Neimay activity in that account.*

Other checks in the same account referred to the hidden Kitty Dunes Heights subdivision. I knew for a fact that we had nothing to do with Kitty Dunes Heights or ADORS. *I was only concerned about the Neimay activity in the account.*

And it took us over seven years of continuous efforts to get this "incomplete" bank information.

It bothers me now that my son's Sea Ox was docked at Nunemaker's wholesale place in Hatteras the day he disappeared.

It bothers me that the district attorney tried to stop my SBI efforts to get the hidden estate account by suggesting my SBI case be closed.

It bothers me that the district attorney's brother was later indicted for drug dealing while driving the DA's car. The brother is from Avon.

It bothers me that the district attorney, when voted out of office, went to work for that same attorney friend of mine from Elizabeth City who sat through the trial all three days.

It bothers me real bad that they are all related, one way or another, to Edgar Styron, Jr., the last person to see my son alive offshore.

It really upsets me that Edgar Styron, Jr. was too busy that fateful afternoon to help get the search started for my son because he *had to go to Avon* with Harry. It was late when he arrived back home.

CHAPTER 16

THE JUDGMENTS – REQUESTED BY JUDGE
March 6, 1991

At the end of the trial, when both sides rested their case, the judge told O. C. Abbott and John Morrison, to draw up a judgment and send it to him. He said if he didn't like either, he would write one himself.

John Morrison wrote him a cover letter stating, "As always it was a pleasure to appear in your court. I look forward to our continuing personal and professional relationship." WARMEST PERSONAL REGARDS, John S. Morrison

I was certainly unaware that John had a personal relationship with this judge that scared him to death. John had acted as if he only knew him only by reputation. For a fact, John was terribly intimidated by him.

O. C. sent in a short judgment that said,

"Wherefore, it is ordered that the accounting requested by plaintiff is hereby denied."

LADIES AND GENTLEMEN OF THE JURY

I DON'T KNOW WHAT THAT MEANS TO YOU BUT TO ME IT MEANS O. C ABBOTT. SAID WE DIDN'T GET THE ACCOUNTING AND WE'RE NOT GOING TO GET IT EVER!

The judge chose the defendant's short little judgment instead of our nineteen pages one. The *only* and I mean *only* part the judge changed in O. C.Abbott's judgment was -

SHIRLEY MAYS

"Wherefore, it is ordered (1) that *upon conducting an accounting as requested in the complaint*, the court determines and decrees that the plaintiff shall recover nothing from the defendant".

What bothers me here is that this special judge started this trial by saying he knew nothing about accounting but when the defense said we couldn't have an accounting, the judge said in his opinion that we already got it.

LADIES AND GENTLEMEN OF THE JURY

Is that *SHOOTING FROM THE HIP* or what? I rest my case and smell an appeal.

CHAPTER 17

THE VERDICT – BY "SPECIAL" JUDGE
March 7, 1991

I need to make a few corrections.

First the judge is not special. His letterhead says recalled. So from now on, I'll refer to him as the recalled judge. It is sad that someone more familiar with the lawsuit couldn't have heard this case but when you're dealing with a judicial system that rides the circuit – you don't choose the horse.

I don't believe this recalled judge studied any exhibits – because he asked if either attorney wanted to take them home. I doubt that he read the depositions either.

John Morrison said at the time that he had never seen anything like it.

I don't believe this recalled judge had to do any consideration after the trial was over.

One of the orders in Mr. Abbott's judgment that they both agreed on was and I quote:

That the plaintiff be taxed with the cost of court.

LADIES AND GENTLEMEN OF THE JURY

Are we talking justice or what?

CHAPTER 18

APPEAL AND FORMAL COMPLAINTS
March 9, 1991 - May 7, 1992

It was a real busy time for me right after this judicial sandbagging.

Centura had really intimidated John Morrison. His Elizabeth City office was in their bank.

I couldn't let him off the hook. I had nowhere to turn at this point so I instructed him to go forward with the appeal. It was "hit one and pull John." I actually was daring him not to go forward.

At the same time, I started my formal complaints to the regulatory bodies. They were the only watchdogs the public had in the State of North Carolina.

1. The Federal Bureau of Investigation
2. The Internal Revenue Service
3. The CPA Ethics Board, a Regulatory Agency to Protect the Public
4. The Banking Commission of the State of North Carolina
5. The Financial Crime Division of the State Bureau of Investigation
6. The Attorney General for the State of North Carolina
7. The Director of the State Bureau of Investigation
8. The Fraud and Abuse Division of the State Auditors Office
9. The Legal Division of the Real Estate Commission
10. American Institute of CPAs, New York, New York

If you will notice, the only group I did not inform was the North Carolina State Bar. Why waste my time?

At the time, I was reading a lot in the press about white-collar crime and it's effect on our country.

The USA Today Opinion was that white-collar felons belong behind bars.

Their article said that white-collar criminals are robbing us blind and too many of them are getting away with it. They are lining the pockets of their three-piece suits with $200 billion a year. (*And this was in 1985* – when we filed our lawsuit.)

Violent criminals, the ones we really fear, steal much less - $11 billion a year.

What is a white-collar crime?

They said it is money laundering. It's fraud. It's rip offs. It's check kiting.

The article said white-collar criminals who break laws jeopardize companies, endanger banks and push up prices for all. Last year (1984) criminal acts played a part in more than half of the USA's bank failures. If you burgle a house or steal a car, you will probably go to jail. But, if you commit your crime in a boardroom, it is likely you'll just pay a fine and take a little ribbing at the country club.

THERE SHOULD BE NO DOUBLE STANDARD.

White-collar criminals deserve what the constitution demands – equal justice under the law. END OF ARTICLE.

On March 9, 1991, I contacted the FBI in Charlotte, NC and later met with their two top agents. One was in charge of drugs and one was in charge of political corruption. I filed a formal complaint with them that I suspected a white-collar crime in Dare County, which involved drug dealing.

On March 11, 1991, I put in writing to John Morrison that the Mays did not feel they got a fair trial and we wanted to appeal. I specifically told him of my concern of the original Planters Bank checks that were seized, bonded and put under the care of Betty Mann, the Dare County Clerk of Superior Court. I realized the recalled judge said the restraining order should be dissolved and the checks returned to the defendants but I wondered if the matter should be addressed legally since we were going to appeal.

On March 22, 1991, Jack Neighbors, the executor sent a letter and a package to O. C. Abbott asking him to please read the contents and keep copies. He asked for a *direct mailing address* for Mr. Mays. That seemed foolish since I was right there in town and Bud was not even in the State of North Carolina. He left the state directly after the trial. Besides, Neimay was my problem now and John Morrison knew it. In the "little brown envelope" to Mr. Mays from Jack Neighbors was a letter expressing the regret the suit had cost them so much *BUT THAT IS BEHIND US NOW*.

He enclosed the 1989 and 1990 tax returns, which had been requested by Shirley Mays for over a year. Jack Neighbors said that Tom White advised him to get Mays' signature on a small designated *PARKING LOT* in Kitty Dunes West, which was an issue remaining to the final dissolution of Neimay.

And a P. S. saying that his wife Carla informed him three weeks ago that they are to be separated and she will seek a divorce (after 17 years).

On March 25, 1991, O. C. Abbott wrote John Morrison and said he would appreciate it if he would forward these documents on to *MR. MAYS PERSONALLY AND NOT TO SHIRLEY*.

His "little brown envelope" already had postage on it and he doesn't even know where Mr. Mays is? Does this sound like Mr. Abbott is still in the strategy of "DIVIDE AND CONQUER?" He must not feel victory yet!

By the way, as coincidences go, I just happened to be in John Morrison's Centura office and notice the "little brown envelope" on his desk. He said he needed Bud's address. I asked why? *John was caught. I think he had crossed over by then*. He was about to do their dirty work. He knew I had Bud's power of attorney. *He had drawn it up.* And besides - any Neimay assets were mine now. *He also drew up that agreement.* I told Morrison *not to worry.* I would call Bud right then from his office and get permission for me to have this "little brown envelope." I did and Bud did and -

LADIES AND GENTLEMEN OF THE JURY

Once more it's touché Mr. Abbott. *So much for divide and conquer.* I really think O. C.'s huge signature goes with his strategy. Elementary psychology 101.

I still have that "little brown envelope" involving *THE PARKING LOT.* I've kept it by my Bible all these years – just waiting for the right time to talk about it or *maybe write a book about it.*

On March 28, 1991, John Morrison sent me a letter telling me he was going ahead with the appeal.

On April 8, 1991, I wrote Debbie Burgess, who had now willingly become a part of the problem, and acknowledged receipt of the Neimay 1989 and 1990 taxes. We had been double taxed on the divided lots and receivables. I sent them back to her because they were not correct and we didn't want to become any party to wrongdoing with the IRS. She had marked the 1990 one FINAL so I reminded her that according to Jack Neighbor's letter, accompanying those returns, Neimay was not dissolved yet because of *THE PARKING LOT.*

I HAVE NEVER HEARD FROM DEBBIE BURGESS SINCE. WONDER WHO SIGNED THE NEIMAY IRS TAX RECORDS FOR 1989 AND 1990?

On April 15, 1991, I made a formal complaint to Ms. Suzanne Battles of the Department of the Treasury, Internal Revenue Service, in Memphis, Tennessee in regard to the hidden estate account that Jack Neighbors was using and Betty Mann was ignoring. I took the IRS individual and address directly from the estate folder so I am sure she was the proper person to contact about that estate. I told her it was not being reported to the state or federal governments. She later answered my letter and said she checked and was told it *was not enough to worry abou*t. *WONDER WHO TOLD HER THAT*? Did they inform her of the second estate account and how long it was hidden from the government? Guess the federal government doesn't care if it only involves several hundred thousand dollars. I think it depends on their source of information.

On May 8, 1991, with the help of my accountant Doug Hollowell, I filed a formal complaint against Debbie Burgess. I reported an ethics violation, which dealt with retention of client's records.

On July 30, 1991, Morrison wrote me confirming a visit in which he had given me the transcript of the trial. *I had paid for it in advance.* He then stated that he did not feel that he could *ethically* represent us in the appeal with a legal reason why the verdict should be overturned. I found out he had given a copy of my transcript to O. C. Abbott *TWO WEEKS BEFORE HE GAVE ME MINE!*

Where were John Morrison's ethics then?

He later justified his actions by saying he had called Bobby James to be sure he was making the right ethical decision. Mr. Bobby James initiated the bar disciplinary committee and the client security fund which reimburses people who have been defrauded by lawyers. It is interesting to note that Mr. Bobby James resigned in September 1992 when his records were being probed. *It appeared to be a matter of ethics.*

SO MUCH FOR LEGAL ETHICS!

On July 31, 1991, I filed a formal complaint with the State of North Carolina Banking Commission. They were very nice people and wanted to help but I was told they didn't have the "rules or regulations" to deal with this type of request. I just thought GOOD GOSH – where do you go in the State of North Carolina to report a white-collar crime? They did the best they could but nothing developed.

On August 1, 1991, the FBI gentlemen I met with wrote that it appeared no further investigation of officials at the former Planters Bank, Manteo, North Carolina is warranted – *inasmuch as the statutes of limitations has run and prosecution under these circumstances is impossible.* (Forget the research legal students. There is your answer.) They also said there is no federal jurisdiction under which the FBI can conduct an investigation into the disappearance of your son, Jeffrey, as there has *never been any evidence* developed in that case.

Maybe law enforcement didn't develop any evidence but I have over 23 years of investigation involving many of them.

On August 8, 1991, I received a letter from John Morrison in which he answered many of my questions, especially about O. C. Abbott getting my trial transcript before I did. He said and I quote, "When I received the transcript, I made a copy for myself since the original would have to be filed with the court of appeals. I then allowed O. C. to make a copy of my copy. I did this to defray possible expenses in the event of an adverse ruling by the court of appeals."

AND THAT MAKES IT OK FOR JOHN MORRISON TO DO THAT WITHOUT MY PERMISSION – TWO WEEKS BEFORE I GET IT? AND THEN WITHDRAW. NOT IN MY OPINION.

LADIES AND GENTLEMEN OF THE JURY

- How lousy and lame was that *ethical* excuse?
- Shouldn't John have asked my permission before giving a free copy of the trial transcript to the defendant's attorney – two weeks before he gave me mine – because of a possible adverse ruling later? It was my property. I paid for it.
- Had he already made his decision about the appeal results before the appeal was even filed?
- At the same time – not good timing Morrison – he informed me he is withdrawing from the appeal. Whose side was/is he on?
- Are these serious life changing court cases just a game for the attorneys?

WHAT GOES AROUND COMES AROUND

I had asked for an appeal immediately after the trial was over. As I said, John was hard to find and hard to push at that point. He was unfamiliar with the new legislation that had been passed and he was three days late in filing the appeal. It was really a coincidence that I was in the local post office when my cousin, who works there, said "Shirley, you have a letter from John Morrison without postage. Do you want to pay it?" How about that timing? John was informing me of his withdrawal which was to take place in two days in the nearby county of Currituck. They put postage on Bud's mail – in advance not even knowing what state he was in - but John left it off mine and I was right there in his town. I would imagine John was aware that it wouldn't be delivered without postage! *I don't think he wanted me to attend.* After seven years of working together on this case, I think a personal phone call would have been more in order.

Not knowing what kind of judicial trick they were going to pull this time, I really wanted to attend the event. I went and took a witness – a friend of mine from out of town.

Judicial joke it was! This hanging was held in Currituck County in a quaint little courtroom with nobody present but the judge, O. C. Abbott, John Morrison, a *TAPE RECORDER*, my friend and me. When I arrived and John saw me, his face turned blood red and he started pacing the halls. I *think* down deep he felt badly about what he was about to do but when the entire judicial system is coming down on you, you have to make a decision. *John was making his decision that day.*

The judge and O. C. Abbott just joked around the entire time. My friend and I and the tape recorder were their only audience. We didn't think they were as cute as they thought they were. Then John Morrison, their main player, took the stand.

John asked to be released from the appeal process and the judge allowed me to protest. I just said, "Your Honor, can you tell me where the Appeals Court is located?" He turned to O. C. who was sitting beside him in a little hardback chair and said, "O. C. do you know that address?" O. C. said, "No sir, your honor but I will get it." The judge then said OK and give it to *her*. He then pointed to me.

The judge gave Morrison the *three days* he was late on the appeal, allowed him to withdraw, gave me thirty days and these words of wisdom –

"LITTLE LADY, IF I WERE YOU, I WOULDN'T LET ANY GRASS GROW UNDER MY FEET."

My friend and I were very embarrassed for them but I could already feel the grass growing.

Little did they know that I had already been to Raleigh – done my homework at the Legal Library – and had written my Writ of Certiorari. An attorney friend of mine who was well aware of their antics told me what I had to do. I couldn't even pronounce it and I had to write one. After I finished it, the same attorney told me that it was darn good. It's amazing what you can do without counsel when pushed to the wall.

My thirty-day extension request appeared to be a problem for the Appeals Clerk. I was told it is usually automatic for attorneys. The Appeals Clerk wanted to know the name of my attorney. I had a strong feeling he had a distaste for people without counsel.

I again wrote Special Agent Melinda Coffin of the SBI. She had said in her letter to the district attorney in 1987, that if any criminal activity were indicated, she would be happy to investigate the matter further. I wrote to tell her of the hidden estate account that was not reported to the state or federal governments.

Out of total frustration, I wrote the Honorable Attorney General Lacy H. Thornburg and said, "What does one do, with hard evidence, about a white-collar crime involving a prominent bank, a prominent law firm, two CPA firms and a real estate company, if it cannot be exposed within the legal system of the First District of the State of North Carolina?"

I didn't really expect to hear from the attorney general so I called his office to ask, "How do you get rid of a district attorney?" As soon as the answering party, Mr. Rodney Maddox, pulled himself up off the floor, he said, "What did you say?" I repeated myself. He simply said, "I don't know." I asked him to please research it and send me the statute. A couple of days later I received the statute in the mail.

I received an order from the North Carolina Court of Appeals denying my Motion for Extension of Time. John Morrison had assured me that the thirty-day extension was routine and he had never known one to be denied. *Another first for the layman.* That privilege must only apply to attorneys. I did exactly what he suggested and I was denied.

I forgot to mention that I had gone to the Fraud Division of the State Auditor's office. They evidently were impressed with my documentation because they put me way up on their list in front of many of their other cases. They came to my home on the waterfront in Elizabeth City a short time after my visit to Raleigh. I was making a formal complaint against the Dare County Clerk of Superior Court because of her lack of action against the hidden estate account. The fraud men left my house and drove directly to Dare County. *SOMEBODY OF VERY IMPORTANT POLITICAL INFLUENCE MUST HAVE INTERCEPTED THEM.* Before they could get out of Manteo, Betty Mann had scheduled me back in her court.

As I said, never underestimate the power of politics.

At this point, I got hit with a biggie. Just when I thought I had figured out where all the political shots were coming from, I got a letter from the Department of Marine Fisheries in Morehead City, North Carolina. It said they were *SORRY* they were just now getting around to my claim. *What claim?* I had no idea what they were talking about! As I read on, I realized they were talking about a 21 year old statute that had never been enforced – having something to do with my waterfront property in Elizabeth City where I lived – and which they referred to as *SUBMERGED LAND*. The attorney general's office would be involved with this ruling.

GOOD GOSH AGAIN. I SHOULDN'T HAVE CALLED THE ATTORNEY GENERAL'S OFFICE ABOUT GETTING RID OF THE DISTRICT ATTORNEY. I THINK THEY ARE REALLY MAD--------BUT SO AM I. THIS OUT OF CONTROL POLITICAL POWER IS RIDICULOUS.

Then I got a letter from the same Rodney Maddox in the attorney general's office who had sent me the statute about the DA. He said, "You may also be assured that I am providing your correspondence to the attorney general for his *personal* attention."

I was well aware of the attorney general's personal attention of me.

I needed a CAMA permit. That stands for Coastal Area Management Act. I had been working on regulatory permits for my Elizabeth City waterfront property for about six or seven years – side by side with the Neimay lawsuit in Dare County. All of those regulatory state officials had been in Raleigh several years working for the Democrats. My waterfront property just happened to be a pet project for the present Republican Governor. Unfortunately, Governor James Martin had kept a lot of the Democrat staff after he got in office. He was an educator – not a politician. He had to learn political hardball the hard way. I advised him to watch his backside because his staff was undermining him.

Governor Martin brought a lot of powerful people to Elizabeth City for a special meeting with me to review my permit situation. The permit required a change in the administrative procedure and a change for the Corp of Engineers in order for them to work together. The Chief of the Regulatory Branch of the Corp of Engineers, Wilmington, North Carolina was at that meeting and he wasn't happy that I was in possession of a letter of his which stated, "if that project goes, there would be lawsuits all over the Coast of North Carolina."

It was obvious they had *DENIED* other people building permits and in some cases, had even torn their properties down. The Chief of the Corp of

Engineers had been able to delay me for years – before Governor Martin stepped in.

The good governor later quit politics with time remaining in his term. The attorney general, same one, had called for a criminal investigation on him. It blew the governor's mind and he quit – saying he despised politics and the attorney general. He also had received some personal attention. That attorney general had plans to run for governor. I'm telling you some of these politicians and law enforcement people are hardball. They abuse their offices. They can destroy you.

I think it is interesting to note that shortly after that meeting, the Chief of the Regulatory Branch of the Corp of Engineers in Wilmington, North Carolina retired from the Corp and went to work as a private consultant working *with* developers. He later told a developer friend of mine that he was sorry he had caused so many people so much hardship. He said he didn't have the rules and regulations to do what he did.

Of course he had no idea he was talking to a friend of mine. *In fact, I was the one who had recommended him to my friend because of his "knowledge."* I knew about that remark the same day. So much for the six or seven years of hardship he had caused me. *He was sorry? So was I.*

This unexpected shocking letter from Marine Fisheries about this SUBMERGED LAND PROGRAM gave me exactly 90 days to defend my title. John Morrison had been the attorney for the seller of this land in 1977 when we bought it and he never mentioned that he had registered a claim for the seller. *Nothing had followed the deed to the courthouse about this statute.* Nothing showed up in the title search. I was fully insured by a title insurance company. We, the buyers, had not been informed of this statute by the closing attorney, John Morrison.

Grass was also growing on my 90-day deadline for defense of title of my home.

I immediately went to the local courthouse to start my research. I saw O. C. Abbott at the Register of Deeds office and he told me I was working him to death. He had just submitted a Response to Plaintiff's Petition for Writ of Certiorari with the Court of Appeals in Raleigh in response to my WRIT. I immediately pulled my tongue back into my mouth and tried to look rested. *Actually, I was totally exhausted trying to stay ahead of them.*

I got a real nice reply from Charles Dunn, the new Director of the SBI in which he stated that he was responding to my letter to Attorney General Lacy Thornburg. He said he had requested that Special Agent Coffin examine my information to determine if further investigation was warranted.

I then received a call from Special Agent Melinda Coffin of the SBI to say my case had been reopened. *That gave me a little hope.*

Betty Mann and O. C. Abbott hauled me back down to Dare County lower court and got the appeal dismissed. I thought we were dealing with a WRIT. I'm not sure at this point whether anybody's right hand knows what his or her left hand is doing. I was certainly having a hard time figuring it out. I was, of course, without counsel.

What a web we weave --------------------

Let's get back to the land grab from the Division of Marine Fisheries and their boss, the attorney general. What a scandal for the State of North Carolina! John Morrison had researched my title years ago, when we bought the property, so he went to work researching this GS 115-205 and 206 Statute– SUBMERGED LAND PROGRAM. It was his legal opinion that it was unconstitutional and a violation of the Fifth and Fourteenth Amendments.

I never said John Morrison wasn't smart.

No one knows much, if anything, about this Submerged Land statute. It was enacted in 1965 and closed out in January 1970. Supposedly, you had to register your submerged land. I'm sure property owners thought the registration protected them.

Nowhere in the title search that John Morrison did for the sellers of our property did this General Statute 115-205 show up. John Morrison and I knew absolutely nothing about what they were talking about. *At least John said he didn't.* He had registered the land for them and researched the title for us. I had no way of knowing about this statute or the fact that it might be a lien on my waterfront property.

At the last minute of the deadline in January of 1970, 10,000 claims came in and it blew the minds of the state officials. I was personally told this by Mr. Wojciechowski, the Director of the SUBMERGED LAND PROGRAM. This Submerged Land Program involves 10,000 coastal properties from the Virginia border to South Carolina. This provided a valuable list of 10,000 coastal properties, their owners and addresses. Some people in Marine Fisheries and the attorney general's office had a lot of knowledge of coastal land for over fifteen years before any action was taken. Actually, I believe it could become a federal issue. John and I made a trip to Raleigh to see the Republican Governor and John informed him of that same opinion. The governor indicated to us that he was going to talk with a powerful coastal senator and try to get the statute amended. *Somehow, that never got accomplished.*

To my knowledge, this statute has never been tested in the U. S. Supreme Court. Would be an interesting class action suit, wouldn't it? The director, in writing, also told me adverse possession could not be used involving properties in this program. Sure hope the attorney general informed all of his attorney friends of that restriction.

Adverse possession means just find a piece of property – maybe on a state list of over 10,000 coastal properties - that no one knows about – stroke a deed – wait the proper length of time – 15 years I think, and it is yours.

LAWYERS KNOW ALL ABOUT HOW TO DO THIS. SOME OF THEM ALSO KNOW HOW TO SWAP MARSH LAND FOR REAL GOOD PROPERTY OWNED BY THE STATE.

We had a clear title and title insurance, which should have meant something to the state. We also had a Veterans Administration loan, which was government approved. Marine Fisheries gave me exactly ninety days to defend the title to our property.

Once again I told myself, WHAT GOES AROUND COMES AROUND.

You know. *ENOUGH IS ENOUGH.* On this lovely fall day, I started once again reflecting on my life. It had been a lot of years since our son Jeffrey was last seen by Edgar Styron and Jock McKenzie off the Coast of Cape Hatteras. I now know there was international drug dealing going on out there and a lot of locals were very much involved. In fact, several of those sea captains have been indicted and served time. Other locals have been caught and served time also. *Many have not been caught. Again, they know who they are!*

There are a million rumors about the boys – to this day.

In my soul, I search for Jeffrey twenty-four hours a day – every day of the year – hoping that he is alive and safe somewhere in the world. If this had been one of my girls, I would have been in a mental institution immediately. At least Jeffrey was physically strong and hopefully had a fighting chance out there that day.

Our family needs answers.

IT ISN'T EASY TO LIVE WITH THE UNKNOWN.

I believe many people know something. You would have a hard time believing the steel doors that keep shutting in my face. Jeffrey's Coast Guard search papers are missing from their Archives and History vaults. *I have proof of this.* It took a nice Coast Guard gentleman in the Portsmouth, Virginia headquarters about a week of steady search to find out where the records were kept in Maryland. He had about fifteen boxes sent to him and eventually found out that Jeffrey's November 13, 1980 search records *were missing.* No one even left a slip in there saying who took them and why. He was real shocked and just didn't have an answer. *At least he tried to help me.* I wanted to find out the name of that big vessel out there on that November

13th. It was gone early the next morning – just like the boys. Somebody knows something about it, I'm sure. I thought it might have been one of those modern day pirate ships – like the MR. BIG from Wanchese, North Carolina that got kicked out of Alaska for "piracy."

Then I reflected on the Dare County white-collar crime I had been pursuing since George died in 1983. I thought about all of the political corruption in North Carolina and the lack of law enforcement. And then I thought about those regulatory body people, who, in cahoots with the Corp of Engineers, had managed to keep me from developing my own waterfront property since 1983. I quickly came back to reality and realized where I was and what I had to do.

I intended to search my property back at least 50 or 60 years. I didn't want any problems with the state when I finished. I was lucky that I was in the real estate business and knew how to do this because it would cost me a fortune to hire an attorney to search that far back. It took me a week to research, write up my report and get ready for my trip to Morehead City so I could hand-carry the results. I wondered what all the other poor claimants did who couldn't afford to defend their titles. *They lost it to the LAND PIRATES.* That is what happened!

This wasn't a fair fight at all and I HATE UNFAIRNESS.

I finished my 3" report defending my title and hand-carried it to Morehead City to the Department of Marine Fisheries.

I wasn't impressed with anything or anybody that trip!

Almost simultaneously with the Martine Fisheries and the attorney general's submerged land hit, I got hit with about a 500% increase in my property taxes from the County Commissioners in my hometown. Right out of the blue, they made an example of me.

At this point, I have little doubt that they were working day and night by phone and fax. I also have little doubt that the *part-time county attorney* (who was on my Bank Board) had ready access to the attorney general's office.

Whether it was another coincidence or not, I appealed the unreasonable tax hike.

They held a special closed-door hearing for me. During that meeting, I told the County Commissioners that their part-time attorney *and* the state representative, (who just happened to walk into our closed doors unannounced and unexpected and who was also on the Bank Board where I owned so much money) had better check into this GS 115-205 Submerged Land Statute because it could affect the tax rolls not only in Pasquotank County but in coastal counties all over the state. If this program, enacted by the State of North Carolina, devalued everyone's prime waterfront property – like it did mine – it would have a huge impact on the public tax rolls. Devalue the property and raise the taxes at the same time – what a double hit!

I smelled a crisis on the horizon.

I also suggested they send my new tax bill to the attorney general because no one was real sure who owned my property.

All lawyers should consider conflicts of interest when working for cities, counties, state or federal governments. Those conflicts can jump up at anytime and come back to haunt them, especially if they can't hide behind a government shield.

In November of 1991, the Supreme Court of the United States ruled that state officials who deprive citizens of their constitutional rights could be forced to pay compensation out of their own pockets.

I started making my list. Who knows? Maybe someday this Submerged Land Program will come back to haunt some people.

The good governor had taken my case before the full Council of State in order for me to get the deed to my submerged land bottoms. *I attended the session that day* in Raleigh, North Carolina and I have personal knowledge that the only person in the entire Council of State who had a problem with me receiving the deed was the attorney general. *I got THE DEED.* It cost me fifty dollars. My property was almost totally over the water. All I could think of at that moment was the Chief of the Regulatory Branch of the Corp of Engineers, Wilmington, North Carolina stating in one of his letters, "if that project goes, there would be lawsuits all over the Coast of North Carolina." No wonder he quit.

1992 started out rather alarming. An article out of Raleigh, our State Capital stated and I quote, "North Carolinians were murdered at an alarming rate in 1991 with drugs rivaling domestic violence as the main motive, authorities said. This State is a damned armed camp, said Charles Dunn, Director of the State of Bureau of Investigation. If things continue, we'll be living in one of the TOP 10 most dangerous states by the end of the decade."

That is what I had been telling anyone who would listen and I didn't even have those state statistics.

- I had put in a formal complaint in my hometown against the lack of law enforcement.
- I had seen the drug trade building up on our waterfront – on both sides of my property and I didn't like it.
- We were having murders that were non-partisan and without concern to race but all related to the drug problem.

The trouble is politicians don't want to hear that kind of talk. It isn't good for public relations. Besides, their attitude is *IF YOU DON'T TALK ABOUT IT, IT MIGHT JUST GO AWAY.* It hasn't and it won't. That is status quo thinking.

Drugs are a big national problem and the problem needs to be addressed yesterday.

It is my theory that the little drug people, who aren't the real problem, are looking at these political white-collar criminals and saying if they can do it and get away with it, we can too. Why not? Although I do not agree with their way of thinking, I can understand how they feel.

The buck should stop at the top and to me, that means from the governor and the attorney general down to the top politicians and the top law enforcers all over the State of North Carolina. How do they expect the public to care if they don't?

I started reflecting again. I filed a formal complaint against the lack of law enforcement in my hometown and I got hit with some break-ins at my waterfront shopping center, a lot of vandalism, and attempted intimidation from some of the local political power players.

I had truly taken on the judicial system and a lot of its players with my white-collar Dare County NEIMAY case.

Now I seem to have taken on the attorney general's office, especially their Environmental Department and the Department of Marine Fisheries with what I see as their illegal land grab on the Coast of North Carolina.

Politicians don't like you to rock their boat.

What I really want to do is just search for my son – fulltime.

I don't cry in public – during the daytime – but I do a lot of it at night when I'm on my hands and knees talking to God. I still remain a firm believer that the Lord never puts more on you than you can handle. I thought to myself that he had better review my situation *FAST!*

The next move on behalf of the attorney general was when the State Highway Patrol stopped me. I wasn't doing anything wrong. I was on the way to see my mother in Camden. I was on a country road and I even saw him coming. *NOBODY WAS IN SIGHT BUT HIM AND ME*. It was so blatant that it put me in a state of shock. I drove a big silver 450 SEL Mercedes and I wasn't hard to spot. I said to myself, "This can't be happening – not in the United States of America." Of course, I took it to court. Of course I lost – because the law is always right.

WRONG!!

I appealed and immediately asked for a jury. *John Morrison couldn't talk me out of it this time!* They delayed the appeal for almost two years. The local district attorney's office (same one) offered me several sweetheart deals of plea-bargaining. They needed a way out. I told those sweethearts I wanted a jury.

At my insistence, John let me help pick the jury. I immediately wanted to get rid of one that I thought had been personally selected as the one to hang the jury. I testified and called the Highway Patrolman a liar, which he was. We proved from his own testimony that I wasn't doing the speed he said I was. He didn't have his radar on. Said he didn't have to. He was doing their dirty work and I knew it. I received a unanimous verdict of not guilty. I felt that justice had been served that day and I would never go to court again without a jury.

As soon as I got home and sat on my waterfront porch, a boat went by and a lawyer I knew yelled out – "congratulations on the win in Camden." Darn – I thought – news travels fast in this little hometown of mine! Wonder how many legal bets were on the table with that one? We're talking less than an hour after the trial.

I heard a rumor the next day that *THE ATTORNEY GENERAL* had been in town during the very important "pull her off the road" trial. Nothing showed up in the paper. He was probably just passing through.

CHAPTER 19

ANONYMOUS INFORMER – THE GRIEVANCE

COMMITTEE

I was very active in my hometown community at the same time all of this judicial and regulatory pressure was taking place. When you are active, some people get jealous and choose "to take you on." Especially good ole' boys. Others seem to care and feed you information. I was accustomed to receiving anonymous letters and phone calls.

- The local radio station called me one day to go on the air and talk about anything I found of interest. I had received that statute from the attorney general's office so I started a movement against the district attorney. *Victims came out of the woodwork.* We started a victim's program. I got anonymous calls from law enforcement and lawyers telling me of their support. <u>*They said they couldn't come out in the public because of what it would do to their careers.*</u> I was even "invited" to Manteo so they could give me some courthouse records about the district attorney's car that his brother was driving when he got caught dealing drugs. I wasn't sure if I was being set up so I called a gun dealer friend of mine to ride down with me. I felt a little safer with him along. The person I met was law enforcement. *Their goals were the same as ours.* We wanted justice. The court records "appeared to show" that the judge didn't handle the release of the DA's car properly. I gave the information to the newspaper. *It didn't fly.*

WHY couldn't those lawyers and law enforcement people who anonymously got in touch with me *STAND UP AND BE COUNTED?*

- While I was on the Board of Trustees of Elizabeth City State University, I would get *anonymous phone calls begging me to help clean up the mess at the University.* I did my best. I went public and then resigned because it all became so political. I said I would not be a party to what was going on between the University and Elizabeth City over *THE* "generator" and electrical scams in the area. Elizabeth City was trying to get rid of a big legal problem and toss it to the University. My responsibility as Vice Chairman of the Board of Trustees was to the governor and the State of North Carolina. I stopped a lawsuit for the State of North Carolina but believe me, I got paid back by some of the local politicians.

  Why couldn't those concerned citizens *STAND UP AND BE COUNTED?*

- I received an anonymous letter in the mail from, *I think*, a professor at the University of North Carolina. He said ---

  "Dear Ms. Mays, I have heard that you are looking into "funny business" on the part of Marine Fisheries officials, the mis-appropriation and illegal use of public and private funds.

  Please let me point you in a direction that might bear fruit. Look into the affairs of a member of the Marine Fisheries Commission (*name*) and his relationship and business dealings with a Mr. (*name*) who operates a (*type of business*) in (*City*). (*Name*), in addition to being a member of the Marine Fisheries Commission, is affiliated with the UNC Institute of Marine Science in (*city*). (*Name*) is renowned for his "research" and work in shellfish reseeding and planting and has for several years received public and private grant money to conduct his "research."

  This anonymous writer then proceeded to tell me the entire scheme! He had to be an insider to know the facts.

  Then he said, "*please forgive the anonymous letter but I must protect myself, for my own personal and professional security.* I do not imagine that the State of North Carolina would look kindly upon a whistle blower that did not reflect favorably the UNC system or the political establishment."

He then closed with – "Warmest personal regards and GOOD LUCK."

People never cease to amaze me. This man wanted me to do something about this abuse of public money but he wasn't willing to *STAND UP AND BE COUNTED*. I had already resigned the UNC "system" and taken on the political establishment. I made sure the letter got to the proper source but I felt sorry for the writer and his weakness. I guess he thought it was OK for me to be a whistle blower. I have no trouble following my principles and evidently my reputation proceeded me. Evidently he didn't have the backbone for it.

BUT THE MOST DISTURBING ANOMYMOUS LETTER OF ALL WAS ABOUT MY ATTORNEY JOHN MORRISON. IT WAS JUST DROPPED ON MY DOORSTEPS AFTER THE NEIMAY TRIAL.

It was dated August 10, 1988 – the exact same time John was too sick to prepare for a "complex" trial. My situation became even more complex after reading that letter.

It was a Public Censure that ordered that a certified copy be forwarded to the Superior Court of Pasquotank County for entry upon the judgment docket and to the Supreme Court of North Carolina for entry in its minutes. It stated, "This Public Censure will also be maintained as a permanent record in the judgment book of the North Carolina State Bar."

All I could think of immediately was when we were before "one" of our judges for discovery and John had said that he would probably "pass it on" because he had received a public censure and that made him weak. DARN IT! I THOUGHT!! I HATE TO BE RIGHT IN THIS CASE ABOUT JOHN MORRISON'S WEAKNESS.

John's Public Censure was from the Chairman of The Grievance Committee. The three-page letter contains these warnings:

- At it's regular meeting on <u>July 14, 1988,</u> the Committee conducted a hearing involving a complaint from (a client) saying John Morrison had told him that he had filed a case for him – *and he had not.* Pursuant to Section 13 (10) of the Discipline and Disbarment Rules, the Committee found probably cause. Probable cause is defined under the Discipline and Disbarment Rules as: "a finding by the Grievance Committee that there is reasonable cause to believe that a member of the North Carolina State Bar is guilty of misconduct justifying disciplinary action."

- His conduct in that matter violated the Code of Professional Responsibility (which was in effect at the time of his actions) and the Rules of Professional Conduct (presently in effect). Disciplinary Rule 1-102(A) prohibits a lawyer from engaging in conduct involving dishonesty, fraud, deceit or mispresentation. The very foundation of an attorney-client relationship is built upon the lawyer's loyalty to his client and the client's trust in his lawyer. A client comes to a lawyer seeking assistance in resolving a legal problem. The client relies upon the lawyer to deal with him in a truthful and honest way relative to the client's case. A client's trust in his lawyer is diminished by the lawyer's misrepresentation of the status of his case

- It is essential that a lawyer deal honestly and openly with his client. A lawyer must keep his client reasonably informed about the status of a matter and the lawyer must promptly comply with reasonable requests for information. The client can only make informed decisions about the representation in his case when his lawyer is honest and forthright in his dealings with his client.

- Disciplinary Rule 6-101(A)(3) (Rule 6(B)(3) of the Rules of Professional Conduct requires that a lawyer not neglect a legal matter entrusted to him. As a lawyer, you have an ethical obligation to attend promptly to the legal matters of your client. The client expects that kind of dedication, commitment, and attention to his case.

The three-page letter from the Grievance Committee to John Morrison concluded by saying ----

"Your conduct was unprofessional. It violated not only the letter of the Code of Professional Responsibility but also its spirit. Your conduct was not the conduct expected of a member of the legal profession and an officer of the court. It brought discredit upon you, the profession, and the courts. It damaged both your reputation and the profession's. It placed your privilege to serve the public as a lawyer in serious jeopardy.

How many lawyers in your area have grievances? Lawyers should have to disclose any grievances to you immediately. You can then analysis the situation and make your own decision whether or not it makes a difference to you. Your future dealings with a lawyer could be jeopardized without this knowledge.

LADIES AND GENTLEMEN OF THE JURY

All of my nightmares just came true. We should follow that gut instinct that God gave us but once I became aware of John Morrison's weaknesses, it was too late. He kept assuring us of his dedication to the case and promised us a vigorous pursuit of justice. I don't think he pushed the lawyers and bankers enough in the discovery process. No case should take six or seven years. The Public Censure was devastating to me. I had been trapped by the judicial system for a long time.

I could go on and on with incidents but I'm going to fast forward to 1993.

I left my hometown and went to the Charlotte area to manage the business of a geologist who was an environmental consultant. I worked with him for nine months while I was trying to get my Elizabeth City property closed. *I sold out in Elizabeth City.* I had given my hometown my best shot. I was finished. A couple of the City Councilmen were pulling every trick in the book to stop my closing. *That's public knowledge.*

The real estate contract on my property was contingent on getting the CAMA permit transferred. It had taken me almost eight years to get that permit. My buyer would inherit that one of a kind deed for the bottoms to my waterfront land. Remember, that Corp guy said, "if that permit goes, there will be lawsuits all over the Coast of North Carolina." I don't believe "they" wanted me to close on that property. After nine long months of personally working with the proper party in Raleigh, I managed to transfer my permit and get my property closed.

I told my geologist friend that I was going back to the Outer Banks to search for my son. A couple of days before I left the Charlotte area, I saw an ad in the paper that read RTC Seminar - $35.00. I had heard about all of those S&Ls going defunct and I knew they had a lot of very good real estate. I was going to have a little money to invest and I thought I might like to buy a piece of property that the taxpayers now own. Sounds familiar, doesn't it? Some lessons in life we have to learn more than once.

During the seminar, the presenters asked a lot of environmental questions. I had a lot of environmental experience so I had a lot of answers. After the session, the government dog and pony guy from Atlanta approached me and said, "You should get certified and work with us. You can make lots and lots of money. We need minority businesses." I was a 100% woman-owned business and the government considered me a minority. I sure needed to make some money because the bankers had taken most of mine. I applied and got certified.

This was my first crack at working for the government. I became certified to do all kinds of real estate and environmental consulting. I probably had more practical experience than all of them at the seminar that day.

LADIES AND GENTLEMEN OF THE JURY

I bet you can guess what is coming next!

That's right. Everything I touched was rotten – to the core. I had never seen corruption of this magnitude. It made the Neimay lawsuit look like little league.

I was awarded five exclusive listings on commercial land in the Research Triangle area of Raleigh-Durham, North Carolina. Good land! I had a lot of followers in my real estate world at that time so I wrote those contracts in short fashion. I was considered a minority firm and I was subcontracting for another minority firm. The owners were Afro Americans. One was a Philadelphia lawyer and one was a Chicago CPA. I started asking too many questions– which was a no no – and they breached my contracts.

While investigating them, I discovered five checks in the FDIC public records that were made out to me for almost $60,000 that I *did not receive* and one for $1800 that I did receive. *I got mad again.*

If I didn't receive five out of six checks listed in FDIC public records, how many thousands of other checks were made out wrong and *who* got the money?

I filed a Whistle Blowing Case in July of 1996 in the United States District Court for the Eastern District of North Carolina. I was told it was the only Qui Tam case ever filed in North Carolina. I was assigned *ANOTHER SPECIAL JUDGE.* In my opinion he didn't follow the statutes. The extension had expired when the Department of Justice decided not to join me. My case involves 747 S&L Institutions and over 400,000 properties (assets). At the time of this book going to press, my case is "pending." The Judge won't move it forward and he won't archive it. He just keeps it *IN CAMERA AND UNDER SEAL. It is his court and he'll do whatever he wants to – whether it is legal or not.* He too appears to be shooting from the hip.

Many, many good books have been written about this great S&L real estate robbery. Most of them stated that it was a $1.4 trillion loss to the taxpayers. I don't believe that would cover it because the damages are ONGOING. There are many spin off damages. The contractors (Corporations) that handled all of these properties, with the help of their FDIC bank "oversight," eroded the real estate market in the U. S. and killed the ancestry of these properties at courthouses across the country because of the way they were indexed. Many of those junk loans were securitized and put into retirement and pension funds. *The FDIC declared the loans to be prudent and proper. Most of them <u>are not</u>.* If discovered, the taxpayers will have to buy them back. That will bring another scandal – in the billions. Susan Smith of the Washington Post predicted this in 1992. *I'm predicting it is closer now in 2004. It takes a long time to expose frauds. The wheels of justice grind slowly.*

The damage from the S&Ls is right up there with the Indian Trust Fund damages. Both of them involve the Department of Interior. It is truly an environmental scandal.

I've studied all of the books written about this great debacle. The very best one, in my opinion, with exceptional statistics is entitled *The Mafia, CIA and George Bush*. It was written by Pete Brewton, an award winning investigative journalist with 15 years reporting experience at the Houston Chronicle, Houston Post, and The Economist. I was fortunate enough to talk with Pete Brewton and thank him for writing the book.

In the *Epilogue* of his book, he stated and <u>I quote</u>, "Another reason journalists are still unable to follow the money is that some of the crucial documents that would allow them to do so are not public. Federal and state Freedom of Information acts and open records laws exempt the relevant financial documents from disclosure. In our case the necessary records are the loan documents, particularly the title company disbursement sheets. (Title companies collect the loan money from the S&Ls and then cut checks to all the parties getting money.) These documents, along with the federal and state examination reports – which are also not available to the public – are the "Rosetta stones" of the savings and loan debacle. Any journalist, federal agent or self-styled expert who claims to know what happened to the money without actually having studied the title company disbursement documents and examination reports is shooting in the dark." <u>End of quote.</u>

It took Pete Brewton five years to get the statistics to write that book. *I know exactly how frustrated he feels.*

LADIES AND GENTLEMEN OF THE JURY

I filed my case in 1996 and continue to expand my research center with hardcopies from the FDIC for the last seven years. One day in May 2003, I just decided to find out who in the FDIC was in charge of that closing information. I got the name and called and requested the REOMS database (real estate owned management system).

The lottery odds were better than my chances of getting that Rosetta stone database.

I was told that they had never given it out before. I told them I had read in the Washington Post, Susan Schmidt again, that Wildlife and Fisheries had it. The request had to pass their main office, FOIA and DIRM (Division of Information Management). I had absolutely no thought at all that I would get it.

I then left town to go on to a trip that I had planned to Destin, Florida to investigate a Nature Conservancy scandal. *I had discovered twenty of them in my Whistle Blowing research.* When I returned, the database was there! It backed up *EVERYTHING* I had been researching for the last seven years. I can tell you the who, where, what, when and why of every single one of those 400,000 plus properties. ***Isn't that overwhelming?*** I definitely consider myself, after twenty years, what Pete Brewton calls a self styled expert.

I truly believe I have their Rosetta stone or at least a very big portion of it. I have the FDIC database closing information on all 400,000 assets. I fully understand all of their codes. "They" falsified the records to block the trail of value. If that isn't fraud, what is?

After I went to Destin for my investigation, the Washington Post started a series of articles about the Nature Conservancy scandals. *I was way ahead of them.*

Can you believe that while I was in court pursuing my white-collar crime in February of 1991 – some of these same people were doing their thing over at the S&L – the Great Atlantic Savings and Loan – just a few blocks away? I think that is why so many people were extremely interested in my case. Especially the two attorneys that sat through the entire three-day trial. *They thought I knew then what I do know now!*

Somehow I feel that maybe NEIMAY LIMITED PARTNERSHIP was just the educational background I needed for this Qui Tam case. *Some of the same Dare County attorneys are involved in the Manteo S&L mess.*

(In North Carolina, real estate agents and brokers have to take continuing education courses yearly. A couple of years ago, the North Carolina Real Estate Commission chose to teach a real estate elective course with the objective to help the citizens from being "suckered into" elaborate schemes and further the "fiduciary" capacity as licensees in relating to clients as well as the public at large. The flaming RED BOOK was entitled AVOIDING REAL ESTATE SCAMS AND FRAUDS. It was written and compiled by Robert Miller, who had relocated to the Outer Banks of North Carolina in 1994, from the West Coast. He had spent 25 years of total immersion into all aspects of financial services. In my opinion, he knows what he is talking about. He teaches for the North Carolina Academy of Real Estate. His CASE #1 SCENARIO in the RED BOOK was based on the Great Atlantic Savings Bank in Manteo, N. C. He wanted the readers of the RED BOOK to know that it was only the tip of the iceberg.)

I believe that my Whistle Blowing case involving these S&Ls became a political issue for the U. S. Attorney for the eastern third of North Carolina. The Eastern District covers 44 counties from Raleigh to the Coast. I am quite sure the US Attorney knew about my judicial efforts in Dare County. *I know her personally.* We are from the same area. We attended several functions at Elizabeth City State University at the same time I was Vice Chairman of the Board of Trustees. She is presently very active in the Democrat Party. Her office, along with the FDIC Inspector General's office, recommended to the Department of Justice that they *not* join my case *because it has no merits.*

She has since retired – *BUT I HAVEN'T.*

202

A couple of years ago, my appointed Whistle Blowing judge decided to retire. He wrote a letter to President Clinton. The very next day he wrote back and said he changed his mind. *He said he was soul searching. Parallel to my case*, he was handling a Conoco oil spill in Wilmington, North Carolina. The judge and Conoco *"reached an agreement"* that the case would stay *IN CAMERA AND UNDER SEAL.*

It's the judge's court and he can do anything he wants to – whether it is legal or not.

There were many outstanding Conoco cases all over the nation and they were afraid that this Wilmington one might set a precedent. One potential case was a billion dollar one in California.

The Morning Star in *Wilmington, North Carolina* – which happens to be owned by the prestigious New York Times – was following the Conoco Wrightsboro environmental oil spill story.

People were driving around Wilmington in Cadillacs after the *IN CAMERA AND UNDER SEAL* decision --------------but they were dying. The good judge kept them from talking about it. That's called an *IN CAMERA AND UNDER SEAL* decision.

A local Star reporter and the Raleigh bureau chief had gone to the federal courthouse in Raleigh, North Carolina and asked to see the file even though it was *IN CAMERA AND UNDER SEAL.* But some papers were loose – by mistake - so they wrote a story on what they had read. They wrote that 178 Wrightsboro trailer park residents had received a $36 million settlement from the Conoco oil company. This fine outstanding judge, who held my future in his hands at the same time of this incident, was furious and he decided to fine the Raleigh bureau chief of The Morning Star of Wilmington, and the Newspaper, owned by the New York Times, more than $500,000 to be paid *to the Conoco oil company* for publishing an article that referred to sealed court documents.

Secrecy, when enforced by a federal court, can be an expensive proposition.

But really – taking on the NEW YORK TIMES. That's a big, big barrel of ink!

Of course the New York Times Co. appealed.

The judge's decision to hold the bureau chief and her newspaper in contempt of court is dangerous, unprecedented and probably unconstitutional.

LADIES AND GENTLEMEN OF THE JURY

That's my new judge!

He had demonstrated contempt for a free press and for an open judicial system.

This was a big, big environmental story but I'm going to cut to the chase. Two press freedom groups and nine media outlets – including The Associated Press, the News & Observer in Raleigh, The Charlotte Observer, Dow Jones & Company Inc. and the Washington Post *joined* the Morning Star's defense.

How do you measure that amount of ink? Someone will have to custom build a big, big barrel for it.

The Conoco Inc. case in Wilmington was the first trial to explore the dangers of an octane enhancer called Methyl tertiary-butyl ether --MTBE. And the judge put it IN CAMERA AND UNDER SEAL?

My senior federal judge refused to allow the newspaper to appeal his order and directed the Morning Star reporter to reveal the names to him in writing by October 20, 1998. (He thought some of the victims had talked.) He also denied the newspaper's request that he remove himself from the case. Judges are powerful people!

There was an interesting article in the Morning Star, Wilmington, North Carolina about this Conoco case dated July 2000.

- It was titled ACCURACY AND FAIR PLAY:

It was a judicial amateur hour.

In the full text, which was copyrighted by the New York Times Company, it read and <u>I quote</u>:

It is a very odd thing to sit in a courtroom, knowing that something is plainly nuts but to watch while a federal judge, a handpicked "special prosecutor" and an oil company lawyer carry out an elaborate charade.

And it is distressing to see the federal courts abused because a judge threw a childish tantrum, or as one columnist reported when it happened, got himself into "a monumental snit."

The "prosecutor" was appointed by "the judge" because the country's top lawyer, the attorney general, rejected his demand that the two reporters and the Star-News be charged with contempt. Janet Reno proved that whatever her faults may be, she knows the law. He passionately asked the judge to convict on all counts.

That would be the same judge who filed the charges and hired the prosecutor.

So, I said to myself, brightly, how do you think we're doing so far?

"The judge" pondered all of several seconds at the end and started convicting. No reason to leave the bench to ponder the slippery path he was about to take. He forged ahead. Might there be, he pondered, a probation officer in the house.

Now, you would have a better chance of winning the five-state Jumbo Lottery with one ticket bought at a 7-Eleven in Alaska than finding one there in the courtroom on Friday afternoon. Dadgum. There she was, as surprised as the rest of them that she might be needed, which is to say not at all.

Far be it from me to suggest something was amiss. I would be shocked to learn that the judge, who filed the charges, hired the prosecutor and heard the case already knew the verdict.

He could, but that would be wrong.

All this came out of our coverage of the Conoco Oil –Wrightsboro drinking water poisoning case. The company and 178 residents fought it out in federal court, reached a settlement and Conoco, with as many as 100 such suits pending around the country, asked that the amount - $36 million – be sealed.

"The judge" running what amounted to the Ted Mack Amateur Hour, never bothered to issue an order, to publish it, or to announce such a thing from the bench despite at least four appeals courts rulings.

That would have given the newspaper that had covered the trial an opportunity to protest, and he had had enough of that. Because of all people, "this judge" knew how to seal a settlement properly.

<u>END OF QUOTE.</u>

LADIES AND GENTLEMEN OF THE JURY

The only thing I "altered" at all in that Morning Star article was the judge's name. Surely the New York Times will forgive me for that. My Whistle Blowing case is *presently* in his court – even though it is hanging in the air. I'm sure you can understand, a little better now, how that can happen.

My case is about bank fraud ----747 Institutions. If my new federal judge will cover-up for the big oil companies – *like Conoco* – think what he will do for his bank friends right in his backyard of Charlotte, North Carolina and his bank friends at the Outer Banks.

What do you think the odds are for this judge to ever address my Whistle Blowing case again?

It would be my dream for the Wilmington Morning Star, owned by the New York Times, to investigate my case and once again find some "loose" papers in Raleigh.

My case is *open* but *dead* like the estate of George Neighbors. What are the odds of my exposing them? Probably just like the odds of the five state Jumbo Lottery at the 7-11 in Alaska!

This judge *appears* to be protecting the recently retired U. S. Attorney for the eastern third of North Carolina and certain individuals in the Inspector General's office of the FDIC – *JUST LIKE HE TRIED TO DO FOR CONOCO.*

I DOUBT THAT THE NEW JUDGE AND THOSE BANKERS I AM AFTER LIKE ME VERY MUCH. I DON'T LIKE THEM EITHER.

The Greensboro News Record, another outstanding North Carolina paper, wrote on October 30, 1998 that "by granting Conoco's request "the judge" followed a pattern that has become all too common in product liability and environmental lawsuits. Corporations held to account for the damage they do usually prefer that the news not get out. But this often has the effect of putting a barrier in the way of the victims who seek compensation for their injuries."

In July of the year 2000, the Morning Star wrote that the newspaper and the two reporters won a legal victory in the 4ᵗʰ U. S. Circuit Court of Appeals on Thursday when judges threw out civil and criminal contempt convictions for coverage of a lawsuit over groundwater contamination by Conoco Inc. at Wrightsboro.

The court also ended efforts by U. S. District Judge ----------- and Conoco to compel reporter Cory Reiss to reveal the names of anonymous sources that disclosed details of the lawsuit's $36 million dollar settlement.

"We thought from the opening bell that our reporters had done nothing but an excellent job of reporting," said Charles Anderson, the Morning Star's executive editor. "This confirms our belief that federal judges must obey the law."

LADIES AND GENTLEMEN OF THE JURY

How do I get so lucky? The judge in question isn't pushing my case either way. As I said, it is just hanging in the air. IN CAMERA AND UNDER SEAL. Delay, delay, delay and KILL. How can he do that legally?

BEEN THERE – DONE THAT. JUSTICE DELAYED IS JUSTICE DENIED. AGAIN.

I've got the closing information on over 400,000 properties in my research center and many of them are environmental scandals all over the United States. Several of them are in Dare County.

I retain a Denver attorney who worked for the RTC/FDIC. He just happens to be an environmental attorney. I hired him in 1997 at the suggestion of Susan Schmidt, investigative reporter at the Washington Post. He had been in charge of closing the S&Ls west of Denver. *He certainly knows the facts because he was an insider*. He is a Whistle Blower himself. He has testified several times in front of Congress. He left the FDIC – sued

208

them – lost –appealed – and lost again. Some of us never learn, do we? He is very courageous.

He was one of five RTC Whistle Blowers who testified at the same time before Congress. One of the other five RTC Whistle Blowers was the lead investigator in the Whitewater scandal. They were willing to <u>Stand up and Be Counted</u>.

I'm not sure Congress even cares about all of this bank fraud. I wonder why?

I just got a Christmas card from my Denver attorney. He is a wonderful, professional Christian attorney. He currently has a case in litigation for a park ranger against the National Park Service. He said in his card, "the agency continues with its mean spirited, shrill defense. I have had it with loud obnoxious arrogant lawyers." He closed by saying, "Have a blessed Christmas. Here's to God's plan for all of us in 2004."

I still retain him. I love this attorney and I am fortunate he came into my life. He and I are just little people. *We need some hardball players.*

I am now meeting with some hardball players. The attorney in Atlanta who referred them to me said they are "Superstars." In the July 2002 edition of the National Law Journal, they are recognized as the fourth most successful law firm in America for JURY VERDICTS.

There is one thing about this new firm that I really like. They always insist on a JURY. And another thing, they have an outstanding environmental department.

CHAPTER 20

NOT THE END OF THE STORY

Actually I started writing this book in November of 1995. There are very few changes. I just put it on a shelf waiting for the right time.

In 1989 an undercover agent gave me three letters that were dated in July of 1987. They involved an announcement from a special agent in West Virginia who sent out an alert to all North Carolina Law Enforcement Agencies. It was asking for any agency having information about a white male believed to have drowned in a boating accident approximately eight years ago to contact him. He was answered by a Captain Leary in the Police Department of my hometown of Elizabeth City. The special agent told the Elizabeth City Captain that a concerned citizen, wishing to remain anonymous, told him that one of the subjects was living in Kodiak, Alaska.

THIS WOULD BE SEVEN YEARS AFTER THE BOYS WERE REPORTED MISSING. WOULDN'T YOU THINK THIS WOULD BE IMPORTANT ENOUGH TO TELL THE FAMILIES?

Captain Leary of the local police told him from the information he was sending that he was referring to the young man who was missing with my son Jeffrey. Leary then wrote Rodney Midgett, Chief Deputy in the Sheriff's Department of Dare County, Manteo, North Carolina (letter missing). Midgett then wrote the Coast Guard at Buxton, N. C. The Coast Guard wrote Midgett back and somehow, this very important incident just fizzled out at the Dare County level.

We were not contacted by any of those law enforcement people. And I know Captain Leary real well.

I consider the situation *VERY IMPORTANT.* Thank God some undercover agent cared enough about our family to give it to me in 1989.

I went to West Virginia to meet that special agent but he would not give me any information because I didn't have an "open case." He told me to contact the FBI.

In 1995, I went to Chapel Hill and met with some literary people. I wanted to expose some folks. My book was too complicated then and more like a classroom study for law, accounting or real estate students.

After leaving Chapel Hill, I decided to swing by Kitty Hawk on my way to Wilmington and visit with a couple of my childhood friends. They are like family to me and have nurtured me for a long time. They always save a few local Outer Banks newspaper clippings if they think they might be of interest to me. Well, they hit the jackpot this time!

The Virginian Pilot had captured a picture of a big vessel, the Mr. Big that had been kicked out of Alaska for "piracy." Mr. Big is three decks high and 165 feet long with a crew of 15. Mr. Big is the largest vessel based at the Outer Banks. They had spent 34 days cruising from Seattle through the Panama Canal and back to Roanoke Island – the Land of the Beginning. They arrived at Oregon Inlet around NOVEMBER 13, 1995.

They had traveled almost 7,000 miles.

Mr. Big had been a former supply ship for offshore oil riggers when the Daniels family bought it. They re-rigged the boat and sent it out to sea. Before coming back to the East Coast, they were fishing off the Coast of Alaska. "We were only working in federal waters, so we didn't get an Alaska permit, Daniels said." On February 16, 1995 Alaska Gov. Tony Knowles said Mr. Big had been "exploiting a loophole in state and federal fishing regulations" and demanded that the pirate fishery be stopped immediately. Knowles urged federal authorities to halt the "bandits."

"There's no right in this deal. The National Marine Fisheries Service didn't even have a scallop plan until Alaska started complaining about us," Daniels said. "I was glad to leave if they ain't gonna let me make no money" said Daniels, who wears a gold hoop in his left ear and has a close-cropped salt and pepper beard and merry Carolina blue eyes.

I thought the MR. BIG might make a good cover for my book since I was going to talk about Outer Banks Piracy. I knew the photographer Drew Wilson who works for the Virginian Pilot. He had taken many excellent pictures of our Coast Guard Station over the years and had been kind enough to give me some negatives from time to time. I waited until I got back to Wilmington and gave him a call. I asked him if I could have a copy of his Mr. Big picture. He seemed pleased to hear from me and said "Shirley, where are you now?" I told him Wilmington. He asked why I wanted it and I said I was writing a book. He asked what it was about and I said my missing son.

About this time, I was put on a speakerphone so I said, "Drew, why did you put me on your speaker phone?" He said, "My editor would like to talk to you." His editor spoke up and said, "I'd like to interview you about your book." I told him I hadn't even finished it yet. Drew said he would get me the picture and we hung up. I didn't know the editor and hadn't even finished the book. I was pleasantly surprised at his interest.

A couple of months went by and no picture. I called Drew again and *he said he sent it*. He told me he would get me another one and send it right away. I received it in a couple of days. As I looked at the picture, I saw three people on the top deck. I wondered who they were. I went to the copying shop and got the best blow up I could. I felt sure one of them was my son, Jeffrey.

I had only shown this picture to one person in Wilmington (Carolina Beach at the time) who was doing some electrical work for me. He knew the Outer Banks well and did a lot of deep sea fishing there with friends. He asked if he could borrow the picture to show to one of his friends. I said yes. I asked the name of his friend. Wow – it was a young man who was a best friend of my son's at East Carolina. My son's friend had called several times during the search. I had not met him so I asked the electrician if he thought the young man would talk to me. He said yes. I made a visit to meet Jeffrey's friend. He and his brother own a fishing company at Carolina

Beach. He's a very nice young man. His brother told me they deal with the Daniels family in Wanchese.

That was *BEFORE* I called and ask for the negative.

I was trying to keep my cool but I really needed that negative. *I called Drew again*. Things had changed. He said the editor had rules and he couldn't send it. He said lots of people come in asking for things like that – lawyers, law enforcement, even Marine Fisheries.

BINGO! I felt I had rung some bells!! Why would Marine Fisheries be interested in that picture? I was working at the time with Missing Persons and we could have used the negative for details to try to positively identify Jeffrey.

Here we are November 13, 2003, exactly 23 years since my son was last seen.

In November of 2003, I visited a restaurant in Elizabeth City and met a man I'd wanted to meet for over 23 years. I shocked him by saying, "What do you know about my son Jeffrey?" He appeared very calm and remembered details as if it were yesterday. We had a nice conversation. I learned two new things. The man I was talking to told me he was "over" Edgar Styron, Jr. at the time of my son's disappearance and that my son and his friend were at Edgar Styron Jr.'s house that fateful morning before they all went out to sea. I had found out earlier that the young man missing with my son knew Edgar Styron well.

I already knew that Edgar Styron, Jr. had told Jock McKenzie on November 14, the day after the search started, that the "boys were OK." Jock McKenzie owned the boat that Edgar was running that day. The name of the boat was EASY RUNNER. Jock had bought it from someone at Pirate's Cove. He later sold it to Edgar. I know this because Jock McKenzie said it in front of a special agent from Missing Persons and me. We had requested a meeting with Jock and had gone to his home near Hatteras to meet him.

I've tried for years to meet Edgar Styron, Jr. I think he is deliberately avoiding me. He seems to always be gone when I get there – wherever it is. I've never seen him. I wish he were not so afraid of meeting me. I just want to ask him some questions.

In November of 2003, I also met with a friend of mine who had been a Coast Guard undercover investigator at the time of my son's disappearance. He has a great interest in Jeffrey's case and has since 1980. I had not seen him since I left Elizabeth City in 1993. I showed him the picture of the Mr. Big. I showed him a blowup of the 3rd deck and pointed to a person who looks like my son.

This friend of mine said he was on the Coast Guard detail that kept that vessel under surveillance for a long time. The Mr. Big had been kicked out of Alaska for "piracy". They tracked it through the Panama Canal. They had the manifest. He said once that vessel docked in Wanchese they checked it the next morning. The next morning one person was missing from the ship. We talked for about two hours. He said, in an excited voice as I was leaving, "I feel certain that was your son."

Was it Jeffrey? Why would he be on that vessel? If so, why haven't we been told by someone? If the Captain of the Mr. Big was just giving him a ride home, why wouldn't they want us to know? Where was Jeffrey's friend? Why wouldn't Jeffrey be able to contact us? Has he been threatened? He was only 21 that fateful November 13 of 1980. He had never been in trouble. What could be so bad as to keep him from his family for 23 YEARS! Does Jeffrey know too much about what was going on that day offshore to be able to come home?

Somebody knows something.

That is why all of those steel doors keep closing in my face. I pray to God everyday that they will tell us. I know that the Lord's timing is perfect. I live for that day.

WE LOVE YOU JEFFREY

YOUR FAMILY MISSES YOU

PLEASE COME HOME!

PICTURE OF MR. BIG 3RD DECK

Through the Panama Canal and on to Roanoke Island

WEDNESDAY, NOVEMBER 15, 1995

DREW C. WILSON/The Virginian-Pilot

The 165-foot commercial fishing vessel Mr. Big, owned by Wanchese Fish Co., approaches the Herbert C. Bonner Bridge at Oregon Inlet last week after steaming 32 days from Alaskan waters. It is the largest vessel based at the Outer Banks.

Wanchese boat returns from Alaska

"The worst part of the trip was the last mile," says captain.

BY LANE DEGREGORY
STAFF WRITER

WANCHESE — Mr. Big is back.

Three months after a judge upheld the closing of the ocean around Alaska to scallop trawlers, the only boat fishing in those waters has returned to Wanchese.

Three decks high and 165 feet long with a crew of 15, Mr. Big is the largest vessel based at the Outer Banks.

The floating seafood processing factory and its fishermen spent 34 days cruising from Seattle through the Panama Canal and back to Roanoke Island. They arrived at Oregon Inlet last Friday.

Capt. William "Punk" Daniels said he plans to spend the next five months refitting his huge boat before sending it to South America where fewer rules dictate commercial fishing practices.

"We traveled almost 7,000 miles to get back here. And the worst part of the whole trip was the last mile," Daniels said Tuesday from the top deck of Mr. Big, which is docked at the North Carolina Seafood Industrial Park.

"I thought we were gonna lose this boat in our own Oregon Inlet. Hell, I was scared. We went about one foot at a time," said Daniels, a 49-year-old Wanchese native who has traversed that inlet hundreds of times. "She don't draw but 8 feet — and we got stuck on the sand bar coming through. I'm surprised we made it at all. That inlet got even worse since I left."

A former supply ship for offshore oil riggers, Mr. Big first arrived on the Outer Banks in 1989. Daniels' family purchased the vessel to add to their fishing fleet at Wanchese Fish Co. Workers re-rigged the boat, added two 15-foot dredges and sent it to sea.

The boat trawled for scallops off New York, New Jersey and Massachusetts for two years. In 1991, the crew cruised to Alaska to drag for scallops off Pacific shores — where the shellfish are considerably larger. Until 1994, Mr. Big carried a state permit for Alaska that allowed its crew to fish up to three miles off the coast and a federal permit that covered waters up to 200 miles offshore.

Please see **Boat,** *Page B3*

220

Boat:

Continued from Page B1

In January, Daniels decided not to renew the state commercial fishing permit because Alaska officials were imposing strict quotas limiting how many scallops could be caught. Instead, the captain relied on a federal permit and only fished between three and 200 miles offshore. Mr. Big's crew unloaded their catch in Washington state this winter — where there is no scallop fishery and, therefore, no scallop quotas.

Daniels shipped almost all of the scallops back to the East Coast.

"We were only working in federal waters. So we didn't get an Alaska permit," Daniels said. "There were 10 other boats scalloping in Alaska waters with state permits. But we were the only one working exclusively in federal waters. We stayed out 35 to 50 days at a time and landed in Seattle."

On Jan. 26, Alaska officials closed their waters to scallop fishing. The annual state quota had been met in less than a month. Mr. Big kept fishing in federal waters.

On Feb. 16, Alaska Gov. Tony Knowles said Mr. Big had been "exploiting a loophole in state and federal fishing regulations" and demanded that the "pirate fishery" be stopped immediately. The governor admitted that "the vessel does not fall under state jurisdiction" because it was fishing outside Alaska's limits. But Knowles urged federal authorities to halt the "bandits."

The North Pacific Fisheries Management Council, which regulates fishing in federal waters, called an emergency telephone meeting about Mr. Big the next day. The group voted to close U.S. Pacific waters to scallopers. A week later, the U.S. Commerce Department enacted the emergency closure.

"They said we were catching five tons of scallops a day. Heck, we only got one ton a day," Daniels said. "They shut the whole ocean down just for our boat. It's mindboggling. The state of Alaska did everything they could to get us out.

"If that's not discrimination, I don't know what is."

In March Mr. Big's owners filed a lawsuit at U.S. District Court in Elizabeth City, asking the U.S. Commerce Department to repeal the unprecedented emergency closure.

In August, a federal judge in North Carolina upheld the Commerce Department's decision.

"There's no right in this deal. The National Marine Fisheries Service didn't even have a scallop plan until Alaska started complaining about us," Daniels said. "They got scallops so thick up there that they can't even find enough food to feed themselves."

For six months, Daniels waited at a Seattle dock for word on the judge's ruling. Mr. Big dragged for scallops off Washington state three times. But the beds didn't yield enough shellfish to justify the trip's expense, said the captain.

So early in October, Mr. Big headed for home.

"I was glad to leave if they ain' gonna let me make no money," said Daniels, who wears a gold hoop in his left ear and has a close-cropped salt-and-pepper beard and merry Carolina blue eyes.

By early spring, Daniels said

workers will have replaced Mr. Big's two generators with machines twice the current size. They'll add 10 wooden bunks to the sleeping births. And they plan to install mechanical shucking machines which have been outlawed in America.

Mr. Big will cruise to Argentina, where Daniels' brother, Apple, runs a 185-foot scallop trawler called the Aaron Bruce. A 30-man crew — about half of whom will be Americans — will live and work on Mr. Big. All the scallops caught in South America will be shipped to East Coast fishing markets in the United States.

"We can only get a permit for Argentina for a year at a time. But we're spending a half-million dol-

lars refitting there. So we Daniels said. shucking mac crease our proc We'll probably instead of dre American scall than those off

Although he Big and called lac of the ocea plan to be on leaves for Arge

"I've been enough," said wife is expect know who will ain't gonna be be back home.'

EPILOGUE

This Neimay case is truly **the tip of the iceberg** involving Outer Banks real estate development corruption. I didn't realize how much until writing this book and studying the depositions of the Neimay characters and re-reading the trial transcripts, Volume I and Volume II. I read them on January 14, 2004. The book was already in its final draft.

George Neighbors may be deceased but he reached out and touched a lot of people before he departed. George took in *limited partners* to feed his greed. *We were not his only victims.* He treated partnerships like his own personal businesses. He embraced bankers, lawyers and accountants and made them a part of his greed. He taught them the game. There was enough money for everyone as long as you stayed on the team. And believe me, it was and still is truly a reality in the real estate world. You can play as long as you don't rock the boat. All it requires is COMPROMISE on your part. To me, that is like selling your soul.

The game is fraud and deception. As long as you don't get caught, anything goes. The part of the game that makes me real mad is when they "use" the judicial system to cover up. The judicial system should be fair and balanced. It should be all about JUSTICE and not about cover up. These Neimay game players used the court to their advantage.

Since it was an accounting case, there were a LOT of numbers. False numbers. That was the essence of this crime. They falsified the numbers to block the trail of value AND GOT BY WITH IT. They want you to look at the numbers until you go blind. They throw a lot of numbers at you – whether they have any meaning or not. The people who tried to cover up for the defendant had to realize what was happening. I believe the judge did also. I was convinced of that after rereading and studying the depositions and the trial transcript.

Based on those legal records and *hindsight,* I want to explain to you what I think really happened in the quaint, historic Dare County Courthouse on the waterfront in downtown Manteo, North Carolina on February 18, 19 and 20 of 1991.

George W. Neighbors – the general partner

First, you have to have a scheme. In this case, it involved land contracts – "unrecorded" land contracts. They are not safe for anyone – the buyers or *limited partners*. Always record your important land purchases and any other important papers.

Let's put a *general partner* in charge of this real estate scheme. In this case, it was a realtor. Then you bring in lots of people. You get the suckerfish first – the *limited partner* and his money. Then a lawyer, then an accountant, then bankers. If nobody rocks the boat, everybody can make lots of money. This scheme is called GREED. If the suckerfish was not a party to this and finds out he has been caught, he has two choices – go along with the plan or fight them and suffer the consequences. In this case, the *general partner* died before the partnership dissolved. The wrongdoing was investigated and the executor was taken to court. The facts were well presented.

It was discovered that the *general partner* was guilty of the following actions plus:

- Commingling bank loans and partnership money in and out of many accounts so as not to be able to follow the trail of money.
- Making a habit of check kiting.
- Making loans improperly to the partnership – charging interest.
- Receiving loans improperly from the partnership – with no interest.
- Having the accountant make up false loans to satisfy adjustments to the books.
- Having the accountant make false adjustments with collection fees, interest, false discounts, etc. in order to balance the books.
- Underselling property and land flipping the same day.

- Not recording land contracts therefore leaving no recorded evidence of sale.

- Failing to keep settlement statements and other necessary records.

These were just a few of the problems that were discovered. It didn't appear to be enough for the judge.

John B. Neighbors, Jr. – the executor

John, who is called Jack, wasn't really a bad son. He just had a bad role model for a father. Jack tried very hard for many years to do the right thing about this case. He just didn't have anyone who felt the same way. His father "involved" others in his deception more than he did his son. Therefore, Jack was kept pretty much in the dark. If there was a second victim in this case, it was Jack Neighbors. He lost his wife of 17 years after this trial through divorce. He lost a lot. *So did we*.

Norman W. Shearin, Jr.- the original Neimay attorney

This was a savvy lawyer from the beginning. *And he is savvy now.* He drew up the original partnership agreement. It would have been okay if George had followed it. From day one, he didn't. This partnership involved 45 acres of prime real estate that was being "administered" by Peoples Bank and Trust Company in Rocky Mount, North Carolina. The property ran from ocean to sound. Very good land! It was priced at $450,000. *The suckerfish was the only person who put money into the deal.* The $50,000 he supplied was used against the $450,000. That left a $400,0000 mortgage. The land was to be released a little at a time. They call that a "release deed." It's done a lot on the Outer Banks. If the releases are handled properly, it is acceptable. Many times in this case, it wasn't.

At the same time of the Neimay Partnership, Norman Shearin, the original Neimay attorney, was in business with Tom White, the Neimay attorney who replaced him and Ray White, President of Planters National Bank and Jim Perry, an Outer Banks realtor in a venture called Sea Ventures. Does this constitute a conflict of interest? What would the priority be for these people once there was a Neimay lawsuit involving the estate of the *general partner* and his many personal Planters Banks loans?

Jasper L. Adams, original Neimay accountant

Jasper is called Jack – Jack Adams. In the beginning, there was Jack Adams. So in the beginning, Jack "appeared" to be part of the awareness. George evidently kept him happy until they went into business together in a partnership called ADORS. *Then George suckered Jack Adams.* Jack was caught up in the scheme. George and Jack Adams had a falling out. Then George died. Then Jack Adams took over the books and managed them the way he wanted. He hid the inner workings of his partnership with George, *(ADORS)*, from the estate. He also hid it from the accounting firm that purchased his business. He hid it from the federal and state governments. He hid it from the executor until the **limited partner's agent** found it in discovery in September of 1988. *Then he made an adjustment to the estate for 1983, 1984, 1985, 1986 and 1987 for ADORS and submitted it on November 10, 1988.*

In my opinion, Jack Neighbors didn't have a clue as to what was taking place for several years after his father's death.

After George's death it got worse for Jack Adams. It appears he had to falsify records to block the trail of value of Neimay money in order to cover for the figures of the partnership attorney's settlement statements. I was told he lost his license during this time. He sold his firm either before, after or during the time he lost his license. When the new accounting firm became involved and became recognized as the Neimay accountants, they chose to "support" only one side – and we weren't on it. *They were not bad people.* They had just bought some bad records and were given bad advice. At that time, the new firm had a choice to be part of the solution or a part of the problem. It appeared to me that they chose to be a part of the problem.

At some period during this time, I was told that Jack Adams was on the Board of Directors of Planters National Bank.

W. Ray White, President of Planters National Bank, Manteo, NC

There are bankers, and then there are bankers who are also developers. This particular banker didn't seem to remember or recall, under oath, very much about the Neimay Partnership even though he had been in a separate real estate venture with the two Neimay partnership attorneys.

Chris Payne, Vice President, Planters National Bank, Outer Banks

And then there are personal bankers.

Meadow Austin, Operations Officer, Planters National Bank, Manteo, NC

I truly believe Ms. Austin got caught up in this mess without her knowledge. She trusted a lot of people who were not trustworthy. She played a key role in this lawsuit because she was the Planters Bank official to oversee me while I was copying all of those third or fourth generation microfiche copies. She was also the person responsible for the automatic transferal of Neimay money out of our account and into Jack Neighbors real estate escrow account. I feel sure she was only following orders. That $40,233.75 Neimay money was used for an improper closing with Billy Beasley, a fisherman. The *limited partner* did not sign the deed.

Today, a huge bank sits on that Neimay property. They need to check their title.

That particular closing was the beginning of a big fraud. The buyers got caught up in the process. I doubt seriously if the buyers had any idea what was happening to Neimay money. That was not their responsibility.

I believe Ms. Austin was innocent of wrongdoing.

Douglas A. Hollowell, the CPA for the Plaintiff

Accountants don't come any better. He and I and John Morrison tried hard to expose the accounting fraud. We were just three against the system. There were *many* of them.

Debbie J. Burgess, partner of Johnson and Burgess

As I said before, I don't think Debbie Burgess is a bad person. She just bought some problems.

Under oath, Debbie Burgess stated that she became responsible for the Neimay accounting on February 15, 1986. She withheld Neimay documents from our accountant and us because she said they were not "strictly called for by the court." *She got bad legal advice from someone she was trusting.*

On May 8, 1991, after the trial and with the help of my accountant Doug Hollowell, I had filed a formal complaint against Debbie Burgess. I reported an ethics violation, which dealt with retention of client's records.

In July of 1991, Mr. Edgar Johnson, who is a partner in the firm of Johnson and Burgess called Doug Hollowell to ask him if he had anything to do with the formal complaint against Debbie Burgess. Edgar Johnson then said, "Debbie Burgess is pissed with Shirley Mays and she is thinking of suing her." He said to my accountant and I quote – "I've been on that Board in Raleigh and I can tell you this case will be dropped." GUESS WHAT? HE WAS RIGHT!

I would like to quote from a letter dated February 6, 1992 from the North Carolina State Board of Certified Public Accountant Examiners – Robert N. Brooks – Executive Director. "Board staff and legal counsel met, at length, with Edgar Johnson, CPA and Debbie J. Burgess, CPA, regarding the above-cited matter – Case #915-014." Further, it says "As the Board staff discussed in the meeting with you and Mr. Hollowell, the issue which appears central to the Board's jurisdiction in this matter is the retention of client records. While a CPA does have a responsibility to return client records upon demand, this requirement is viewed in conjunction with a CPA's obligation to maintain client confidentiality. Ms. Burgess' statement affirms that neither she nor the firm had ever received any document, which indicated that you had been given authority to act in your husband's behalf. Our records do not contain any evidence which would indicate that Ms. Burgess or the firm was provided with a power of attorney by you, your current CPA, or your attorney."

The last sentence stated, "For your information, Mr. Jasper Adams has applied for reinstatement."

I wonder if Ms. Burgess and Mr. Johnson thought the court was that inefficient. This was a six-year lawsuit. The power of attorney had been the first record filed. Otherwise, the plaintiff's agent would not have been able to represent the **limited partner** for six years. Did Ms. Burgess ask O. C. Abbott, Jack Neighbor's attorney, about the power of attorney since she seemed to be followed his legal advice? He had a copy. She never asked us for the power of attorney. That affirmation in Raleigh with the State Board was a desperation move on their part. It worked.

Never underestimate the POWER OF POLITICS – especially right after the judge has ruled against you.

Thomas L. White, Jr., the Neimay attorney "replacement"

Tom came aboard in 1977. Or that is what he stated in his deposition. In his deposition, on September 12, 1986 at 10:00 a.m. in the office building of the executor, he stated that his practice was devoted primarily to commercial and real estate law. He said it was about 75% real estate and real estate litigation. It was stipulated at the beginning of the deposition by John Morrison and agreed to by O. C. Abbott that Thomas L. White, Jr. was indeed an expert in North Carolina real estate transactions. .

Tom was with the Kellogg law firm. It was and probably still is a powerful political force on the Outer Banks and in the State of North Carolina. They have a lot of political influence. They have changed partners *MANY TIMES.* In court, under oath, Tom White offered the following when asked what firms have you been associated with. He said and I quote:

- Originally with Kellogg and Wheless,
- Kellogg, Wheless and White,
- Kellogg, Wheless, White and Reeves,
- Kellogg, White and Reaves,
- Kellogg and White

- Kellogg, White, Evans and Sharp
- Kellogg, White, Evans, Sharp and Michael
- And now Kellogg, White, Evans, and Gray

At the time of trial, they were Kellogg, White, Evans and Gray. The following attorneys were in their firm:

- Martin Kellogg, Jr.
- *Thomas L. White, Jr.*
- Charles D. Evans
- *E. Crouse Gray, Jr.*
- *Ronald E. Deveau*
- *Benita A. Lloyd*
- Lee L. Leidy

Tom White was asked in his deposition on September 12, 1986 "Did you know of any other attorney that was doing work for the partnership during that time that you were dealing with the partnership?" He answered, under oath "I was not aware of any others than within my own firm." It appeared to me that day in court that if Tom went down, he wasn't going alone.

By his own admission, the Kellogg firm was the chosen firm of George Neighbors, and did all or at least the majority of the Neimay closings. By everyone's admission, under oath, settlement statements just didn't exist because that is how they did business on the Outer Banks at that time. Or at least, that is what O. C. Abbott, the attorney for Jack Neighbors said in court that February of 1991.

Referring to these non-existent settlement statements, Jack Neighbors was asked, under oath, by John Morrison, "What would be the reason for handling the transactions that way as you have just described rather than for a more formal presentation?" Jack said under oath and I quote "Avoidance of attorney's fees." Morrison said, "That's a terrible thing you're saying, you know that?" Jack answered, "A capital sin, I believe, punishable by having to do this." (Referring to the deposition).

Jack Neighbors was absolutely right. I had no trouble at all proving that Tom White "appeared" to be deliberately hiding his attorney's fees. They were either cash, grouped together on the wrong settlement sheets (once they "reconstructed" them) or cleverly paid some other way. Tom White's settlement statements "appeared" to show some false figures or either Jack Adams the CPA picked them up and falsified them or BOTH. I think both. *Remember, I have documented proof of all of this.*

Tom White looked out for Tom White first and Planters National Bank second. When he closed those four infamous closings, **Olds, Beasley, Ryder and Anderson,** after George's death, he deliberately broke a lot of rules in order to pay off a personal note at Planters. I believe the buyers were unaware of this.

Tom White had been on the Managing Board of Planters for several years.

The SMOKING GUN was the $40,000 personal Planters' note of George Neighbors and how it was handled. It is my opinion that Tom White broke the following rules while closing four of the Neimay closings after the death of George Neighbors, the *general partner*. **All after June 23, 1983.** This was at the same time that the *limited partner* was desperately seeking information from him.

- A couple of these settlement statements were duplicated and contained conflicting information.
- At least one of these settlement statements contained commingled tax information.
- He withheld Neimay money improperly - $5000 from several closings – and put it in the Trust account of Kellogg, White, Evans, Sharp and Michael – for Inheritance Taxes due arising out of George W. Neighbors Estate. When asked under oath if this $5000 was deposited in his trust account, he said, "I don't believe it was." *It clearly was.*
- He withheld Neimay money to be paid to Peoples Bank & Trust Company for release price *after* the mortgage had been paid off on June 23, 1986. *Where did the actual money go?*

- He sent Neimay money to Planters National Bank for a personal note of George Neighbors. When asked, under oath, had he done that, he said, "No, I don't believe I have. I don't recall that I have." *He clearly did.*
- He provided titles to these buyers without the signature of the **limited partner**. *Wouldn't an expert tax lawyer realize the requirement of the signature of the **limited partner**?*

Conspiracy is a plot. Collusion is a secret agreement of cooperation for an illegal or deceitful purpose. So while Tom White was "improperly" handling Neimay money from the four infamous closings and others, Jack Adams was falsifying the same figures on his accounting to cover it up. Jack Adams tried hard to "adjust" the amounts that Tom White's settlement sheets showed as being paid to Peoples for release - but the mortgage had been paid off on June 23, 1983. The Neimay books clearly showed that. Jack Adams had to record the amounts somewhere so at times he showed them as "loans" to George. Other times, he just took the figures, falsified them and put them under the wrong columns - intentionally.

What would these actions be called if not collusion and conspiracy?

O. C. Abbott, attorney for the defendant

I have nothing but pity for this man. I realize Jack couldn't get anyone else but it wasn't hard to see the wrongdoing of this group. A cover-up is worst than the crime itself. Even if you're only being "used" as a defense attorney for that purpose. *They owe him big.*

As you all know by now, this was an accounting lawsuit so their best strategy was to confuse the judge with a lot of figures. I say THEY because O. C. Abbott was definitely not alone in his legal fight against us. There was a crowd of people behind their bench. One time I looked over and thought they were having a town meeting. They probably were.

In court, O.C. Abbott was rude, wrong and ridiculous. Since he had no defense, he just sprouted out numbers – numbers – and numbers that meant nothing to anybody. He didn't even understand the numbers himself. *He admitted that several times in court.* We had been given a false accounting and he spent hours referring to the false numbers. The judge must have written down hundreds of numbers and this was a judge who said at the beginning of the trial "I never studied accounting as such." *This was not the time for the judge to start his accounting education.*

They needed to discredit us in order to win. Their strategy was to reverse the situation and try to show us as greedy. They tried hard with their false figures to show we got a 40% return on our money and we should be happy with that. *They didn't care who broke the law.* They wanted to make George Neighbors look innocent so we would look guilty.

O. C. had already tried to discredit Bud Mays who had undoubtedly been a very successful businessman. He took a lot of cheap shots at him so I expected nothing less. When he got to me, he asked about my businesses in Elizabeth City and whether they were profitable. He questioned my ability as a broker. *What did all of that have to do with Neimay?* O. C. tried to discredit us business wise and make us look greedy instead of George. *He knows better.*

When my own attorney had questioned me, he allowed me to give my business background and accounting experience, which was extensive. When John Morrison asked me if I had received any special recognition from business achievement – O. C. objected. The judge overruled him so I was able to put in the record that I was a Business Woman of the Year with a Downtown Business Association in 1987 and Business Woman of the Year with the Chamber of Commerce in 1989. Those recognitions came at the same time I was fighting for justice in Dare County.

But the cheapest shot of all that O. C. Abbott took at me was this testimony on February 20, the last day of the trial. It was at the same time as the questions about all of our businesses.

Mr. Abbott: "You say you bought Nunemaker Fish Company from Mr. Neighbors. He didn't sell you that?
Ms. Mays: "He grossly oversold us that, yes, sir, in 1980."
Mr. Abbott: "Now you didn't buy it from Mr. Neighbors?"

Ms. Mays:	"Mr. Neighbors was the real estate person who sold us Nunemaker Fish Company, and grossly oversold it. Yes, sir."
Mr. Abbott:	"And you got kind of mad with him about that?"
Ms. Mays:	"After we found out the trouble we were in, we went to Mr. Nunemaker himself. I've know him all of my life. I've known him since I was a little girl. And Charles felt real badly about it. And he said he would just allow us to pay interest for a while but his wife would not come down on the price. That was in 1980 – in June of 1980. And as you know, Mr. Abbott, we have a son who has been missing for 10 years. And so from that time on, it wasn't that much of a pleasure for my husband."
Mr. Abbott:	"Did you accuse Mr. Neighbors of your son's death?"
Ms. Mays:	"Oh no. Why would you say that?"
Mr. Abbott:	"Just asking, did you do that? Answer "Yes" or "No"."
Ms. Mays:	"My God, it's never crossed my mind."
Mr. Abbott:	"Did you attribute his death to the purchase of the fish house?"
Ms. Mays:	"Did I say that?"
Mr. Abbott:	"I am asking you. Did you?"
Ms. Mays:	"No. It has never crossed my mind."

It had not crossed my mind *then* but you can rest assured it has crossed my mind *now*. I wonder what O. C. Abbott knew at that time that I didn't.

From my testimony, I meant that George Neighbors had grossly overstated the value of Charles Nunemaker's business because *George* was aware that Charles had been stolen blind in that business and it was on it's way down. It's hard to rely on the books of a cash business or the opinion of the broker who is selling it.

At one time, O. C. *was in practice* with the lawyer friend of mine from Elizabeth City. The one who sat through the trial for three days. The one who defended the druggie who threatened me. The one who hired the DA after he got voted out of office. The same DA who got my case against Tom

White, Jack Adams and the bankers closed. And the one who hired our attorney John Morrison when he "chose" to withdraw from our appeal.

My son Jeffrey's disappearance is not the only mystery in this story.

I just read the depositions and transcript of the trial for the first time since the trial. That's almost exactly 13 years ago. I forgot how cruel O. C. Abbott was to Bud and me.

I want to send O. C. Abbott one message and send it clearly.

I HAVE NEVER THOUGHT MY SON WAS DEAD. THAT'S WHY I WROTE THIS BOOK.

John Morrison, the plaintiff's attorney

John Morrison is a good man. When he couldn't beat them, I believe he joined them. It sure looks like it. I told him so when he went to work for that lawyer friend of mine from Elizabeth City.

He presented an excellent case. He just didn't follow through. I understand he is an excellent Sunday School teacher. I sure hope he teaches that faith and truth are power and I sure hope he's practicing what he preaches. Strength comes from that knowledge.

George M. Fountain, the Neimay trial judge

I believe the judge was smart and attentive. I'm not at all sure he admired them. But evidently they accomplished their mission by throwing all of those false figures at him. Anyway, in the long run, he was true to his name. Even though he had never studied accounting, as such, he definitely SHOT FROM THE HIP and we were in his line of fire.

I wrote this epilogue because it's my right to have an opinion. I believe in the Freedom of Speech and in the Freedom of the Press. I also respect the Court of Public Opinion.

235

I have always tried to live by the following rules and in closing, I want to pass them on to you.

- IT IS NOT WHAT HAPPENS TO YOU IN LIFE, IT IS HOW YOU HANDLE IT.

- ALWAYS HAVE FAITH AND ALWAYS TELLTHE TRUTH. THAT IS *REAL POWER* AND IN THE LONG RUN TRUMPS EVERYTHING.

- SET A GOOD EXAMPLE. THE COUNTRY NEEDS IT.

- STAND UP AND BE COUNTED. IT'S YOUR GOD GIVEN RESPONSIBILITY.

"I rest my case."

ACKNOWLEDGMENTS

For years I convinced myself I couldn't write a book. Then one day I became aware that writing a book was just a matter of talking on paper. I said to myself, *I CAN DO THAT*. The thoughts for this book started shortly after our son, Jeffrey, went fishing on the early morning of November 13, 1980 and never returned. It's a big, big mystery as to what happened to him. We live with the unknown. I actually started putting thoughts on paper in 1995. I then put those pages on a shelf. I wasn't receiving any more motivation at that time. I've always believed that the timing of the Lord is perfect.

Several incidents happened in October and November of 2003 involving Jeffrey. My gut instinct was saying to me MOVE AND MOVE FAST. I typed the first draft of this manuscript in five days.

I want to thank God for my sanity.

I would like to thank my *family and friends* who tolerate me.

I want to thank a couple of my good friends who helped me edit this book.

I want to thank my sister for editing my book. She has written two excellent books of her own. I value her Christian opinions.

I want to thank photographer Drew C. Wilson and the Virginian Pilot for the excellent picture on my front cover of the Mr. Big taken from the Herbert C. Bonner Bridge at Oregon Inlet. Drew's timing was PERFECT.

Another person I want to thank doesn't even know me. His name is Bill O'Reilly. He is a straight-shooter. I was agonizing over whether I should use real names or fictional ones. *MINE IS A VERY REAL STORY*. This wonderful cousin of mine knows I love Bill O'Reilly and his No Spin Zone so he surprised me at Christmas with O'Reilly's new book – Who's Looking Out for You? I couldn't read it fast enough.

My decision was made.

If your story is true and you give your characters a false name, then you are only half a truth-teller. Half a truth-teller I'm not! Besides, *I'm the only person looking out for me!*

I want to share a few of O'Reilly thoughts from his new book. He hits many of my thoughts about the judicial system right on the head but he says it much better than I, so here goes --

QUOTE

"The so-called "justice system" in America is not looking out for you, and you should write that down and read it every day of your life."

"The American justice system is a runaway money train where those without legal credentials are tied to the tracks."

"Everybody involved in the legal system is making money except those whom the system is supposedly designed to protect. No matter how you get involved in the legal system, you will pay. Trust me on this."

"Since I can't stand the unfairness of the legal world and even get stomachaches writing about it, this chapter will be very short. But I want to give you a vivid example of how corrupt the American legal system has become, and how it most definitely does not look out for you or for any other nonmember."

"The only active participants in any criminal trial who are not under oath are the attorneys and the Judge. So the attorneys can say just about anything they want to say."

"In reality there is little enforcement against unethical conduct by defense attorneys."

"Our Justice System is overburdened, driven by money and connections, and sometimes downright corrupt, and few in power seem to care."

AND LAST BUT NOT LEAST O'REILLY SAYS

"It is a cesspool of corruption, even if you win you'll get hurt. I love this country, but I despise what our so-called system of justice has degenerated into. If you're an unscrupulous lawyer, the system looks out for you. If you are looking for an honest day in court, well, you have my sympathy, because you are not likely to get it."

END OF QUOTES

Thank you Bill O'Reilly for the encouragement you gave me through your book.

The Mays definitely got hurt in that cesspool of corruption. Maybe this book will help someone avoid what we went through.

Printed in the United States
19743LVS00006B/61-558